The Cherokee Strip

Its History & Grand Opening

 The Oklahoma Legacies Series

The Cherokee Strip

Its History & Grand Opening

By D. Earl Newsom

NEW FORUMS PRESS INC.
Stillwater, Oklahoma

Published by New Forums Press, Inc.

The Oklahoma Legacies Series, Stillwater, Oklahoma

This book is available at discount prices in bulk quantities. Write New
Forums Press, Inc., P.O. Box 876, Stillwater, OK 74076.

Newsom, D. Earl
THE CHEROKEE STRIP: Its History and Grand Opening
(The Oklahoma Legacies Series)

Printed in the United States of America

ISBN: 0-913507-27-X

Table of Contents

Preface and Acknowledgments .vii

1. Why the Strip Was Created 1
   The Cherokees Are Driven West
2. The New Cherokee Nation 9
   The Trail of Tears Leads to Oklahoma
3. Cattlemen Invade the Strip 15
   The Live Stock Association Takes Over
4. On to the Cherokee Strip! 23
   The 1889 Land Run Stirs Settlers
5. Preparing for Opening 29
   Rules Are Set for the Great Land Run
6. The Grand Opening 35
   A Day of Triumph and Tragedy
7. Alva 49
   The Vast Empire of Woods Is Settled
8. Blackwell 59
   "The Rock" Endures After 100 Years
9. Enid 69
   "Queen City of the Outlet"
10. Newkirk 81
    Saloons Provide County Tax Base
11. Perry 89
    Thousands Jammed Hell's Half Acre
12. Ponca City 97
    One Man's Dream Came True
13. Woodward 105
    The Pioneers Survive Blizzards and Bobcats
14. The 101 Ranch .115
    "Magic Empire" of the Cherokee Strip
15. Fighting Over the Spoils 123
    The Big Counties Are Carved Up

16. The Strip in Crisis 129
     Farmers and Oilmen Fight to Survive
17. The Years Ahead 139
     Cities Look to Industry and Tourism
18. Reflections From One Hundred Years Ago 153
     Some Eyewitness Recordings
Notes   173
Index   178

Preface & Acknowledgments

THE PURPOSE of this volume is to present an authentic, documented, and concise history of the Cherokee Outlet/Strip, the events that led to its settlement, and a vivid account of the great land rush of 1893. This includes not only the story of how the Strip came about, but a look at conditions today and what the future may hold. With this history is perhaps the most unusual picture collection ever presented of the Strip and its key cities.

Once as I was beginning another historical book, I asked a friend who spends much time reading what he thought was most important in presenting this type of material. Without hesitation, he answered, "Don't tell me more than I need to know. Don't obscure the story with a sea of extraneous facts, impressive as they may be. If I want to know more, I'll look at the bibliography and find out for myself."

I have attempted to follow this friend's suggestions. "Concise," according to Webster, "suggests the removal of all that is superfluous or elaborative." Thus, "concise" may best describe this presentation. It is a thoroughly documented story that brings up to date the Cherokee Strip history, contains a mountain of information not in previous Outlet histories, and yet is told in a straightforward manner with many rare historical illustrations.

Condensing Cherokee Indian history is a difficult task. Volumes have been written about Cherokee life. Within recent years complete books have been published on the origin of the tribe, the Trail of Tears, and Cherokee population trends. From these and many other sources I have compiled facts on the tribe that have a bearing on the Outlet.

Other important sources studies deal with the Outlet after the white man began making inroads on it. These include George Rainey's classic, *The Cherokee Strip,* published in 1933, Joe B. Milam's thorough articles in the *Chronicles of Oklahoma,* and the doctoral thesis of the late William George Snodgrass of Phillips University entitled *"A History of the Cherokee Strip."*

In addition, I pored over old newspaper files at the Oklahoma Historical Society and visited many of the local communities in the Cherokee Strip, studying their county histories, interviewing their pioneers, and gathering material at their museums.

Today counties and cities all over Oklahoma are working to preserve their heritage. Their research and publications helped immensely on this project. Outstanding county histories with memoirs of pioneers were available at Alva, Perry, Ponca City, and Woodward. Local histories have been published at Enid, Ponca City, Perry, Newkirk, and Woodward. Titles and authors are included in the documentation.

To illustrate the aftermath of the great land run, I chose seven key cities. Five of these had been designated county seats. The stories of the other two, Ponca City and Blackwell, were especially fascinating. And one could hardly tell the Cherokee Strip story without background on the great 101 Ranch. I regret that space prevented more detailed information on such important smaller towns of the Strip, such as Fairview, Cherokee, Tonkawa, and Pawnee.

I am most grateful to many individuals throughout the Strip for their help in gathering information and pictures. I delayed pursuing the project until I was assured that historical pictures would be available. The kindness and cooperation of several individuals finally made that decision possible.

Velma and Ray Falconer of The Glass Negative in Ponca City have a vast picture collection numbering in the hundreds of dealing with Oklahoma history. They generously made their Ponca City pictures available for this book. Darrel E. Keahey has a similar collection of early Enid pictures and he permitted me to select those that best depict Enid's early life. Blackwell historical pictures were difficult to find, but Aileene Owens of the Cherokee Outlet museum made available copies of needed prints. Similar cooperation came from Karen Dye, project director of the Newkirk Community Historical Society and from Mrs. Jack (Mary) Erskine, at Alva. Mrs. Erskine not only provided pictures through the Alva Centennial Commission but permitted me to use those from her own collection.

The reader will find in this book reproductions of two very rare paintings, Robert Lindneux's "The Trail of Tears," and John Noble's "The Run." For these I am indebted to Linda Stone Laws, Curator of Art at the Woolaroc Museum near Bartlesville.

Important help came from individuals at other Cherokee Strip museums. These included Clyde and Chester L. Speer and Kaye Bond at Perry, Laura Streich at Ponca City, Bob Howell and Fran Nulph at Enid, and Ron Seamon and Mrs. Vera Strasbaugh at Alva. I am especially thankful to Ron for taking time to locate newspapers from Alva's earliest days that made it possible for me to record the early history there.

A note of thanks is also due those at the Oklahoma Historical Society who were especially helpful. These include William Welge, Chester Cowan, Scott Dowell, Mary Moran, and Eleanore Landon. And also to Darrell D. Garwood and Nona Williams of the Kansas State Historical Society, John R. Lovett of the Western History Collections, University of Oklahoma, and the entire staff of the Audio-Visual Aids department of Oklahoma State University.

A number of readers commented on the maps done by Mike Shores in my previous book *Stillwater - One Hundred Years of Memories*. His maps relating to the Cherokee Strip are even better. Our thanks also to another member of the same city department, Brian Brown, for information on population. Additional population figures came from Jeff Wallace of the Oklahoma Department of Commerce.

The important information concerning agricultural conditions in the Strip came largely from the Oklahoma Agricultural Statistics Service of the Oklahoma

Department of Agriculture. Help in interpreting this information came from Robert M. Reed, retired Oklahoma State University specialist and Duane McVey, Payne County Extension director. Similar help in interpreting oil information came from J. B. Red, a name well known in the Oklahoma oil business.

John Augelli, director of Stillwater's public library, always goes beyond the call of duty to help authors gather bits of obscure but important information. Through his efforts, I was given access to several historical books and microfilm that were very needed. Roseanna Ratliff and Mrs. Gerald Sober helped in a similar manner with information in Ponca City.

Thanks are due two former Stillwater *NewsPress* colleagues, Lawrence F. (Chub) Bellatti and Dale Van Deventer, Chub for memories of his youth in Blackwell that made caption writing easier, and Dale for his counsel and help on production as for previous books. Also leading us to sources on Blackwell history was Dayle McGaha, *Journal-Tribune* general manager.

This is my first publication by New Forums Press, Inc., and I am most impressed by the quality and professionalism of the work they have provided.

And last, my appreciation again to Chandra Davis for typing a sixth manuscript. From everywhere comes advice to get a word processor, but Chandra is much more intelligent and reliable.

D. Earl Newsom

About the Author

A native of Drumright, D. Earl Newsom is author of four other historical books, including *Kicking Bird and the Birth of Oklahoma, Stillwater—One Hundred Years of Memories,* and two volumes on the great Drumright oil field. He is a graduate of Oklahoma State University and Northwestern University, Evanston, Illinois. He began his career as a newspaper reporter and editor and then taught journalism at Texas A. & M. College and the University of Maryland. He has received numerous citations for academic and professional achievement.

Dedication

To Bernice—
A real pal and a wonderful sister
through all the years.

THE COVER: Artist Jack Allred of Stillwater, Oklahoma, is noted for his cover paintings on historical books, and this is his fourth cover for author D. Earl Newsom. The painting reflects some of the memoirs of his great grandfather, Francis Marion (Bud) Dawson, who made the Cherokee Strip run. Mr. Dawson is among those portrayed in the 1893 diary reproduced in Chapter Eighteen.

Chapter One

The Strip's Beginning

Why the Cherokee Outlet Was Created

THE OPENING of the Cherokee Outlet, popularly known as the Cherokee Strip, on September 16, 1893 was one of the great spectacles of American history. Estimates of those making the run ranged from 100,000 to 150,000. Thousands more stood by as witnesses.

As homesteaders lined up along the borders of the vast land which is now in present day northern Oklahoma, the Cherokees were no longer a part of the scene. Yet the opening represented another milestone in the Cherokees' assimilation into the white man's world. It would not be long after this that the Cherokee Nation itself would be dissolved and the Indians would become citizens of a new territory.

Non-historians are sometimes confused by the terms "Outlet" and "Strip." This is understandable. For a time, there existed both a Cherokee Strip and a Cherokee Outlet. The Strip was a band of land only two-and-a-half miles wide that extended for 276 miles along the southern Kansas line. It was caused by conflicting surveys of Cherokee lands made in 1837 after the New Echota Treaty of 1835 and the Kansas-Nebraska Act of 1854. This Strip was sold by the Cherokees to the government after the Civil War and then ceded to Kansas.

The Cherokee Outlet was created in an 1828 treaty to give the Cherokee tribe an outlet to hunting grounds in the West when they moved to the Indian Territory. It was on the western edge of the new Cherokee Nation. After the Strip became a part of Kansas, cattlemen and settlers began referring to the Outlet as the Cherokee Strip. This became the choice in popular usage, although "Outlet" is still historically correct as the name of the land settled in the run of 1893.

Cherokee Origin Uncertain

The Outlet story is a part of Cherokee history. Some highlights of the tribe's history and the events that led to the creation of the Outlet will give readers a greater appreciation of the grand opening.

While there is little doubt the Cherokees were the most influential tribe in

America and often called the most enlightened, neither they nor historians have been able to determine with certainty the tribe's origin. Leading scholars and ethnologists have for the most part concluded the Cherokees were once a part of the Iroquoian family that settled along the shores of Lake Erie and Lake Ontario. They cite strong similarities in the language and traditions of the two tribes. Eventually, the Cherokees became weary of fighting with their brethren and over a long period migrated southward through Ohio and Pennsylvania and settled in the mountainous areas of North and South Carolina, Tennessee, and Georgia.

In later years, this theory has been questioned, and archaeologists have suggested that Cherokee culture has existed in the Southern Appalachians for more than two thousand years, long before the presumed migrations.[1]

Regardless of their origin, the Cherokees found their mountain home ideal. They built villages along the numerous

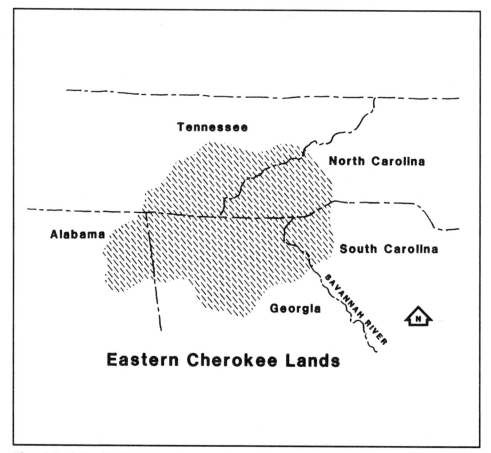

Eastern Cherokee Lands

The origin of the Cherokee Indians has never been definitely established, but evidence exists they may have been in the above area 2,000 years ago. It was from here they migrated to the Indian Territory. [Map by Mike Shores, Assistant Planner, City of Stillwater.]

sparkling streams. Usually in the center was a clan house. Their homes, constructed with a mixture of clay and small limbs, extended from the clan house. On the outer fringes of each village were gardens that produced such crops as corn, sweet potatoes, beans, and tobacco. The Cherokees lived well as hunters supplemented the crops with fish, game, nuts, and fruit. A replica of an early Cherokee village has been created at Tahlequah, Oklahoma.[2]

The Tribe Divides

Not all tribesmen cared for the settled village life. Many who preferred hunting, fishing, and scouting moved to the lowlands and led a more nomadic life. As the separation occurred, those who remained in the villages became know as the Upper Cherokees, those living along the headwaters of the Savannah River were called the Lower Cherokees. Those in between were the Middle Cherokees.

The Cherokees established their capital at Itsati (Echota) in eastern Tennessee on the banks of the Little Tennessee River near present day Madisonville, about 30 miles south of Knoxville. In 1820 the capital was moved to Georgia and called New Echota.

Historians have long marveled at the rapid development of the Cherokees from primitive life to civilized ways, particularly since 1730. Much of this has been attributed to their intermingling and intermarriage with families of Irish, German, English, and Scottish descent who settled on lands near the Cherokees. Such families included such names as Adair, Vann, Chisholm, Ward, Hicks, Reese, Wickett, Fields, Ross, Lowry, and Rogers.[3] Descendants of these families played prominent roles in later Cherokee history.

In spite of their seemingly ideal homeland, the Cherokees found life anything but peaceful and prosperous. Time and again they suffered tragic losses that threatened their very existence. In 1738,

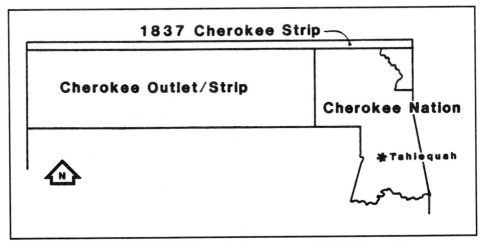

The two Cherokee Strips have been confusing. The first area called the Strip was the narrow band across the southern border of Kansas caused by conflicting surveys made in 1837 and 1854. It was ceded to Kansas after the Civil War. The Strip opened to settlement in 1893 was legally the Cherokee Outlet, but cattlemen and settlers called it the Strip. [Map by Mike Shores, Assistant City Planner, City of Stillwater.]

a smallpox epidemic swept through all Cherokee towns, killing hundreds of tribe members. The Indians had no knowledge of smallpox and tried to drive it away through dances and rituals.

Cherokee Towns Destroyed

But the greatest losses were caused by war. In spite of their adaptability to civilized ways, the Cherokees were fond of war. Often they went to do battle with nearby tribes, and each time many young braves failed to return.[4]

The most devastating war loss came in 1776 during Revolutionary War days. Angered over a land sale, Dragging Canoe, an impulsive young Cherokee chief, provoked an encounter with colonial armed forces. The army struck back with a two-pronged attack that destroyed more than 50 Lower and Middle Cherokee towns and killed several hundred Cherokees. Hundreds of others fled into the mountains or into Florida where they suffered starvation.[5]

In a report of the Bureau of American Ethnology to the Smithsonian Institution, historian James Mooney described the Cherokee disaster:

> More than fifty of their towns had been burned, their orchards cut down, their fields wasted, their cattle and horses killed or driven off, their stores of buckskin and other personal property plundered. Hundreds of their people had been killed or had died of starvation and exposure, others were prisoners...and some had been sold into slavery. Those who escaped were fugitives in the mountains, living upon acorns, chestnuts and wild game. From the Virginia line to the Chattahoochee the chain of destruction was complete.[6]

Before an imminent attack on highland towns, the Upper Cherokees asked for peace talks. A treaty was signed May 20, 1777 in which the Cherokees gave up several thousand acres of their land.

The Cherokees began to rebuild their homes and towns, but by 1808, their situation became so oppressive from whites wanting their land that those in North Carolina, Georgia, and Tennessee sent delegations to Washington to seek relief.

The Move to Arkansas

Lower town delegates said they wished to continue living as hunters but that game had become scarce in their present land. They asked to move west of

Sequoyah, perhaps America's most revered Cherokee, was a member of the delegation that signed the treaty in 1828 in which Western Cherokees agreed to give up their Arkansas lands. The treaty was the beginning of the Cherokee Outlet. [Courtesy Oklahoma Historical Society, neg. #5095.]

the Mississippi River. The Upper town delegates asked to remain in the East.[7] Out of this grew a treaty signed in 1817 by several leading Cherokee chiefs and by General Andrew Jackson and other government representatives, by which the Lower Cherokees traded their eastern lands for an equal number of acres in Arkansas.

Fewer than 2,000 Cherokees moved to Arkansas at first, but through land and annuities provided them they became prosperous and content. Soon they were followed by about 3,000 others. An estimated 10,000 remained in the East.[8] Those who moved became known as the Western Cherokees and those who stayed were referred to as the Eastern Cherokees.

The contentment of the Western Cherokees was short-lived. In 1818, the government obtained from the Osage Indians just west of the new Cherokee home a large tract of land that would today be Adair, Cherokee and Sequoyah counties of Oklahoma, and parts of Muskogee and Wagoner counties. This became known as the Lovely Purchase, for William L. Lovely, a government agent.[9]

White settlers began to move on this land and Arkansas in 1827 made it into Lovely County. The Cherokees were angry because this had been their outlet to western hunting grounds.

The Outlet Is Created

When a delegation of Cherokees, including Sequoyah, went to Washington in 1828 to protest, they were persuaded to sign a treaty agreeing to give up their Arkansas lands and to move to the new Lovely County. Their tribesmen were surprised and angered and even threatened to hang those who signed the treaty, but

Sequoyah built this cabin in 1829 near present-day Sallisaw. It is now enclosed in a larger stone building and part of a state museum. [Courtesy Western History Collections, University of Oklahoma Library.]

this was the beginning of the Cherokee Strip.[10]

To placate the Cherokees, the government included a provision for a perpetual hunting outlet to the West that would extend from their newly assigned home to the western boundary of the United States, which was then the one hundredth meridian.[11] This vast area of more than six million acres was officially designated the Cherokee Outlet but was later referred to by homesteaders as the Cherokee Strip. The treaty wording later resulted in a great dispute. As the U.S. boundary extended further west, the Cherokees felt their Outlet should be extended with it.

The Arkansas Cherokees remained bitter at having their homes traded off, but they began moving in 1829, most of them settling along the Arkansas River and its tributaries north of Fort Smith.[12]

The Eastern Cherokees, meantime, were faring even worse. After the Revolutionary War, American colonists encroached more and more on Indian lands. Pressures grew to move all of the Five Civilized Tribes to the West. In 1824, President James Monroe asked Congress to establish a territory for Indians. The proposal became a reality when President Andrew Jackson signed the Removal Bill in 1830.

1835 Treaty Stirs Hatred

With this action, the government began to negotiate with each of the tribes to get them to leave their homes in the East and to move to a newly designated Indian Territory in the West. The government was especially eager to get the Cherokees out of their choice lands in Georgia.

Up to now, the Cherokees had remained united against white encroach-

ment on their lands, but the treaty negotiations tore the tribe asunder. The large majority of Cherokees were opposed to a removal treaty, but on December 29, 1835, at New Echota, the Cherokee Nation capital, a small group of Cherokees signed a treaty with the government to exchange eastern lands for those in the new Indian Territory. Among those who signed for the Cherokees were Major Ridge, William Rogers, Elias Boudinot, John Adair Bell, and James Starr. Signing two months later were Stand Watie and John Ridge.[13]

The treaty was a milestone in Cherokee history for the Cherokees ceded to the United States all of their lands east of the Mississippi for $5 million. They were guaranteed in exchange for their

Elias Boudinot, educated at Cornwall Mission School in Connecticut, signed the 1835 treaty that forced the removal of the Cherokees to the Indian Territory. He believed it was their only hope of survival, but his fellow tribesmen never forgave him and marked him for death. [Courtesy Oklahoma Historical Society, neg. #13596-b.]

ancient homeland a new home in the Indian Territory already partially occupied by the Western Cherokees who had moved there from Arkansas.[14]

Sixteen thousand Cherokees protested the treaty to the President and the U.S. Senate, with John Ross as their principal spokesman. Ross had been imprisoned on December 5 and held for 13 days to curtail his opposition, but on his release he went to Washington to try to stop its approval. All opposition efforts failed and the Senate approved the treaty by a margin of one vote.[15] The fate of the Cherokees was sealed.

One may wonder why the relatively small group of tribesmen would agree to such a treaty. Elias Boudinot, one of the signers, had been educated at Cornwall Mission School in Connecticut and became the first editor of the Cherokee *Phoenix.*. His name was respected in the East as well as in Europe. Boudinot believed the Cherokees were doomed if they remained in the East and the only hope for their salvation was to move West.[16]

The majority of the tribe did not agree and awaited a chance for revenge.

Although of small consolation to the Cherokees, the treaty confirmed the 1828 treaty granting the tribe a "perpetual and unmolested" outlet to the West.[17] The Cherokees could not live on this outlet, but could use it as a route to western hunting grounds. Thus the corridor later to be known as the Cherokee Strip was assured. For the time being, however, the Cherokees would have to contemplate the more immediate agonies brought on by the New Echota Treaty.

The Cherokee National Capitol Building still stands in Tahlequah. It was built shortly after the Civil War. [Courtesy Oklahoma Historical Society, neg. #2393.]

Chapter Two

The New Cherokee Nation

The Trail of Tears Leads to Oklahoma

AFTER THE New Echota Treaty, pressure grew on the Cherokees to give up their eastern lands. At first, the Indians refused to leave, but several contingents agreed to depart in 1837 to escape harassment by whites. Most of the tribe, however, made no provision for the emigration. They could not believe they were to be uprooted, their homes and property taken from them, and they would then be sent to a distant part of the country.[1]

Reality came soon. In May 1838, 15,000 Cherokees still remained in the East. General Winfield Scott, in command of army troops in the area, told the Cherokees the emigration must begin at once. His 7,000 troops began a round-up of tribal members. Stockades were built to hold them until their departure.[2]

Some Cherokees were seized in their fields and others in their homes. As they were taken away, many looked back and watched their homes in flames and their cattle being taken by whites. Many Indians were held in embarkation camps along rivers. Often they went without food and slept on the bare ground. These actions were the advanced stages of the Trail of Tears which one historian said "may well exceed in weight of grief and pathos any other passage in American history."[3]

The Journey Begins

One contingent of Cherokees embarked on the trail to the West in the summer, but the suffering was so great from the heat that many became ill and died. General Scott accepted a plea from the tribe that emigration be postponed until autumn. The Indians were kept under guard in their concentration camps until October.[4] Then began the Trail of Tears to the Indian Territory.

It has been estimated that during the bitter winter of 1838-1839, as many as 4,000 died during the trip from pneumonia, tuberculosis, and even starvation. Chief John Ross led one group, and his wife Quatie, died of pneumonia in Little Rock, Arkansas.[6]

At the end of their journey, the Cherokees were settled in the northeastern section of the Indian Territory, sharing the land occupied by the Western Cherokees who had been removed from Arkansas. Adjacent to the land on the west was the Cherokee Outlet. Thus, the immigration brought the Eastern and Western Cherokees together again, brought about a new Cherokee nation, and established an outlet for them to hunt in the West.

But before a tribal reunion could occur, an act of vengeance shocked all of the tribe's factions. The Trail of Tears had increased the bitterness of those who had opposed the treaty that forced them to move west. One June 22, 1839, they struck back.

Treaty Signers Murdered

In a well-planned action, assassins killed three of the signers. Major Ridge was shot by a sniper as he walked along an Arkansas road. His son, John, was stabbed to death in their home in the presence of his wife and children. Elias Boudinot was bound and slashed to death with knives and tomahawks. Stand Watie was marked for death, but escaped when he was forewarned.[7]

For a time it was feared the assassinations might cause a civil war within the Cherokee Nation, but the tribe proceeded quickly with a convention starting July 1, 1839 on their Illinois River

An estimated 13,000 Cherokees traveled the Trail of Tears from August 1838 to March 1839. As many as 4,000 may have died en route. This 1942 painting by Robert Lindneux may be the best portrayal of the tragic journey. [Courtesy Woolaroc Museum, Bartlesville, OK.]

campgrounds. There they hoped to organize a new government and to draft a constitution.[8]

On July 12, they passed an "Act of Union" that created a Cherokee Nation and unified the Eastern and Western Cherokees. In September they called a national convention and adopted a constitution and designated Tahlequah as their national capital. John Ross was chosen as principal chief.[9]

In spite of these achievements, the two treaty factions continued their vendetta. Stand Watie blamed John Ross for the assassinations of the Ridges and Elias Boudinot. Ross sought protection from the government as rumors spread that Watie was planning to assassinate him. Murders were reported daily throughout the Nation.

A New Nation Begins

Finally, in 1846, the government sent a commission to seek peace. From this came a treaty signed August 6, 1846, that secured land in the Cherokee Nation for the common use and benefit of all Cherokees and granted amnesty for crimes committed if fugitives turned themselves in by December 1. Among other provisions to temper strife were those awarding $115,000 to members of Ridge's Treaty party for its losses and $5,000 to the Ridge and Boudinot families.[10]

The treaty brought peace for a time within the tribe, and the Cherokees turned to the development of their new nation. Their achievements were astonishing. Again, they proved their ability to rise from tragedy to great heights.

Even before the treaty, the tribe had begun the civilizing of its new Nation. The National Council set up funds for

Major Ridge (above), leading advocate of the 1835 treaty, and his son, John (below), were both assassinated after they moved to the Indian Territory. [Courtesy Oklahoma Historical Society, neg. #5968-a.]

public schools, and these had begun in 1841. Dwight Mission had been moved to the Territory from Arkansas in 1829. It became an educational center for the Cherokees. Other churches and missions were established, and the Cherokees took pride in building their capital city, Tahlequah. Some parents sent their youths to academies outside the Territory.

In May 1851, the Cherokees opened two seminaries for higher learning near Tahlequah. The *Cherokee Advocate*, the first newspaper in Oklahoma, appeared in September 1844.[11] The Cherokees established commissions to promote friendly relations with other tribes. Many tribesmen began to wear white men's clothing.

As the Cherokees adapted to their new home, they found less use for the outlet that provided hunting in the West. Many were devoting their time to raising crops and livestock.

Civil War Begins

In the midst of such prosperity and advancement, the Cherokee bubble burst again. The Civil War began in April 1861. This was a war between whites, but the tribes in the Indian Territory were soon to be involved. The war left most of the Five Civilized Tribes in tatters. It again split the Cherokees into bitter factions, and reopened wounds of the New Echota Treaty and the Trail of Tears.

Most of the tribes aligned with the Confederate forces. Some were slave holders. Others had intermarried with white southerners and were familiar with their culture. The tribes were also virtually isolated from Union forces and under great pressure from Confederate leaders in the area.

Chief John Ross was obstinate and for a time successfully kept the Cherokees from involvement, even after the other tribes had allied with the South.

John Ross, principal chief of the Cherokees for 40 years, traveled the Trail of Tears, and his first wife, Quatie, died en route. With him here is his second wife, Mary. He bitterly opposed the 1835 treaty. [Courtesy Oklahoma Historical Society, neg. #13530-a.]

But in August 1861, Ross yielded to great pressures and recommended that the Cherokees join Confederate forces. This was achieved in a treaty with the South on October 7. This meant the end of relations between Indian Territory tribes and the United States. The die was cast.

In spite of the treaty, not all Cherokees favored the alliance, and in February 1863 a group met at Cowskin Prairie and repudiated that treaty. Thus, the tribe became split into the Northern and Southern Cherokee factions. Each claimed to be the true representative of the tribe. The situation became more complicated when John Ross was captured by Federal troops at Park Hill near Tahlequah. He was taken East and permitted to live in Philadelphia until the war's end.

Stand Watie, Ross' bitter enemy, was elected principal chief of the Southern faction. Watie immediately began to vent his long suppressed hatred on Ross' supporters and Cherokees loyal to the Union. Ross' home was looted and burned, and many other homes were destroyed by Watie and his followers. Watie was one of the first to ally with the South and he rose to rank of brigadier general before the conflict ended.

Thousands Suffer

By the end of the War in April 1865, the Cherokees were in a tragic state. As Union forces occupied Tahlequah and Fort Gibson, the confederate Cherokees fled into the Choctaw Nation or even into Texas. They were afraid to return for they realized the hatred brought on by the New Echota Treaty, which the Ridge-Boudinot assassinations, and the war itself had all greatly intensified. Bitterness between the tribal factions seemed beyond repair.

Thousands of Cherokees suffered from starvation and disease, and many died during the conflict. Beyond such personal tragedies the war would cost the Cherokees a large segment of their outlet to the west and it was the beginning of the end for the Indian Territory itself.

As soon as the tribes had formally surrendered, their leaders were anxious about the future. They asked the government to hold a council to clarify the post-war status of the Indians. The government was eager to resume relationships with the tribes and agreed to the request. Out of this grew one of the greatest Indian councils ever held.

Stand Watie escaped would-be assassins. He later became a Brigadier General for the Confederacy during the Civil War. [Courtesy Oklahoma Historical Society, neg. #12398.]

The Fort Smith Council

In early September 1865 thousands of Indians and their most distinguished chiefs arrived at Fort Smith, Arkansas. They represented most of the plains Indians as well as the Five Civilized Tribes. Conducting negotiations for the government was D.N. Cooley, Superintendent of Indian Affairs.

Cooley told the Indians that because they had rebelled against the government they had forfeited past treaty rights and their property could be confiscated. He said the Indians must give up their slaves. But he said the government wanted them to have homes and that relationships between the tribes and the government should be restored.[12]

While Cooley and his delegation treated the Cherokees as the most important tribe present, he rejected their plea they should be considered as Union allies because of the support of the Northern Cherokee faction. The Southern Cherokees claimed that circumstances forced them to join the Confederacy but this, too, was discounted. Cooley said the tribes must be regarded as a conquered nation and they must negotiate on the government's terms.

Violence almost erupted between the two Cherokee factions as the Commission refused to recognize John Ross as principal chief, and Elias C. Boudinot, now a Southern faction leader, made an impassioned speech accusing Ross of being responsible for the murder of his father, Elias, after the New Echota Treaty.

After eight days of negotiating, Cooley realized he could not complete treaties with the tribes. He persuaded the tribes to sign a preliminary treaty renewing their allegiance to the United States and told them he would negotiate with each tribe separately in Washington in the months ahead.[13]

Outlet Tempts Cattlemen

These negotiations were carried out and the subsequent treaties became known as the Treaties of 1866, in which the tribes made concessions of land that would have great impact on the future of the Territory.

Because of the intense hatred between tribal factions, the Cherokee treaty took longer than others, but it was finally concluded in July 1866. Among its provisions were those granting homesteads for freed slaves, amnesty for all offenses, the end of confiscation laws, and the right of the President to correct injustices or injury between sections of the Cherokee Nation.

One important provision dealt with the Cherokee Outlet. Under Article 16, the government was authorized to settle Indian tribes from other parts of the nation in the Outlet.

Whites along the southern Kansas border closely watched these developments. Since the Cherokees could not live in the Outlet, it was left virtually unattended and now might become isolated from the tribe. The choice grazing lands were becoming a great temptation for cattlemen and homesteaders.

Chapter Three

Cattlemen Invade the Strip

The Live Stock Association Takes over

THE 1866 TREATIES divided the Indian Territory into two sections. Lands sold by the Indians to the federal government became the Oklahoma Territory. Those still occupied by Indians were still the Indian Territory.

After the treaties, life in each of the territories was strikingly different for the next 40 years. Plains Indians in the west continued their savage warfare with one another. The Five Civilized Tribes in the east resumed their efforts toward civilization. As far as the Cherokees were concerned, what to do with their Outlet

The Cherokee Strip was considered a cowboy heaven, and these six in 1884 were with the Comanche Pool, one of the largest operations. [Courtesy Kansas State Historical Society.]

became a problem that lasted for the next quarter century.

Shortly after the 1866 treaty with the Cherokees, the government began to move other tribes into the eastern end of the Outlet. First came the Delawares in 1867. They were followed by the Osage, Kaw, Pawnee, Ponca, Otoe, and Missouria, and Nez Perce tribes. The latter were later transferred to Washington and Idaho and replaced by the Tonkawas.[1]

The Cherokees were happy to dispose of part of the Outlet since it had rarely been used. The buffalo had virtually disappeared and white settlements had mushroomed in Colorado and New Mexico. Their hunting corridor had lain dormant for years. The Cherokees were also in dire straits financially. A failure of their corn crop had left them almost destitute. The government paid the Cherokees 47.49 cents per acre for the estimated two million acres in the area just west of 96th meridian.[2]

As the tribes moved into the Outlet, they completely blocked the entrance from the Cherokee Nation. The corridor thus became virtually useless to the Cherokees, but not to others. A new era was about to begin on these fertile plains.

The East Wants Beef

During the Civil War and in the years immediately following, a great cattle in-

Cowboys often operated out of line cabins from which they rode to tend cattle and check fences. This group is listening to one cowhand's banjo tune. [Courtesy Kansas State Historical Society.]

dustry built up in the Southwest, especially in Texas. In the meantime, the war had left the East cut off from beef supplies for several years and easterners were anxious to get these renewed.[3]

So great was the demand after the war that the cattle business became almost a craze and swept over the entire southwest from Colorado to the Gulf of Mexico. How to get the cattle to the eastern markets became the dilemma for all cattlemen.[4]

They chose the rather obvious route—over the trails of the Indian Territory, through the Cherokee Outlet, and on to Abilene, Kansas, where the cattle were shipped to the East via the Union Pacific Railroad. As the Santa Fe railroad extended its lines southward, Wichita, Caldwell, and Dodge City became busy cow towns. Luxurious grass that grew along the trails provided the cattle sustenance over the long drives.[5]

When drovers refused to pay the Indians for use of their grassland, the Kiowas, Comanches, and Cheyennes stampeded the cattle and sometimes purloined a few head for themselves. Even soldiers could not keep the cattle off the Indian lands and finally the government drew up leases that paid the Indians two cents an acre for grazing rights.[6]

The Outlet Is Invaded

But it was in the Cherokee Outlet the cattle business had its greatest impact. The strip of land contained more than six million acres of the finest grassland. And it was unoccupied.

Cattlemen took full advantage of the situation. In 1866, 600,000 head of cattle were driven across the Outlet. If a ready market was not available, the cattle were kept in the Outlet to graze until it was

About 15 cattlemen belonged to the Comanche Pool, which looked after 26,000 head of cattle. The operation extended from Comanche County, Kansas, far into Woods County in the Strip. The Pool headquarters, above, were west of Medicine Lodge, Kansas. [Courtesy Kansas State Historical Society.]

profitable to ship them. From 1866 through 1884, more than 4,800,000 cattle were driven through the Outlet from Texas alone.[7]

Several cattle trails passed through the Outlet, including the best known in history, the Chisholm Trail, named for Jesse Chisholm, a mixed blood Cherokee guide and trader. It extended from Abilene, Kansas, south through Caldwell and into the Outlet where it followed the course of present day Oklahoma Highway 81.

Along the site now are Medford, Pond Creek, Enid, Kingfisher, El Reno, Chickasha, and Duncan. Eventually the trail extended all the way to San Antonio. It has been estimated that as many as 14 million cattle passed over the trail in herds ranging from 500 to 1,000 in number.[8]

Kansas ranchmen also took advantage of this unusual situation. They regularly drove their cattle into the Outlet to feed on the lush pasture. All of this was done under a vague common law practice called "cow custom."[9]

Cherokees Begin Charging

Finally, the Cherokees decided the use of their Outlet had gone far enough. They began to collect rentals from cattle outfits using their land. The charge was at first one dollar per head but finally was established at 40 cents. The first year's proceeds netted only $1,100, but in 1882, the amount had risen to $41,233.81.[10] Still, many cattlemen paid nothing. Their cattle drifted from one area to another and often were mixed with other herds.

To cope with confusion in the Outlet, cattlemen gathered at Caldwell, Kansas, in the spring of 1880. They discussed grazing and how to protect their cattle in

These Cherokee Strip cowboys are taking time off for lunch and coffee. [Courtesy Kansas State Historical Society.]

a land that had no law or courts. The group formed a loose organization to deal with problems.

In the meantime, the Cherokees had established an office at Caldwell. Their system of issuing grazing permits encouraged many ranchmen to build fences for their cattle. Although the practice was contrary to government rules, the Cherokees approved it because they thought it would make collecting grazing fees easier. Ranchmen often paid Cherokees large sums to use their Indian names in applying for licenses. Soon the Outlet became a patchwork of fences.[11]

Quarrels over fencing rights began almost immediately and after an investigation by the Bureau of Indian Affairs, the War Department was asked to tear down all fences in the Outlet. A storm of protests followed from cattlemen, and the War Department showed no interest in using soldiers to tear down a thousand miles of fencing. After a second investigation, Secretary of the Interior Henry

Teller ruled the ranchmen could keep their fences if they made satisfactory arrangements with the Cherokees.

Live Stock Association Begins

This eased tensions in the Outlet, but on March 6, 1883, cattlemen pasturing herds in the Outlet gathered again at Caldwell, Kansas. The organization they started in 1880 became The Cherokee Strip Live Stock Association.[12]

The association expanded its earlier aims of protecting cattle and included in its purposes improvement of the breed of domestic animals, recording all transfers or ranges, recording marks and brands of animals owned by its members, and a procedure for settling all disputes. It has been called the most powerful organization of its kind in the world. It moved quickly to obtain control of the entire Cherokee Outlet.

Earlier in 1883, the cattlemen had

Not all ranch houses were like those in cowboy movies. This one was in the Cherokee Strip in 1886-1887. [Courtesy Kansas State Historical Society.]

approached Dennis Bushyhead, principal chief of the Cherokees, about a lease
of the Outlet. Bushyhead reacted favor-
ably and in May he called a meeting of
the Cherokee National Council.

With the help of association members, he secured approval of a lease for
the entire Outlet for a five-year period for
$100,000 a year, payable annually. The
bill was signed on May 19 and a formal
lease was completed in July. It went into
effect on October 1, 1883. The Cherokees
insisted the first payment be made in
silver, and $50,000 in silver was hauled
to Tahlequah to meet the demand.

An Era of Peace

While the lease closed the Outlet to
many who still wanted range land there,
it brought an era of peace. The Cherokee
Strip Live Stock Association went to
work to bring the vast strip under control. Each member was granted a five-
year lease on his range. He would pay
one and one-fourth cents an acre every
six months. The member would build his
own fences, camps and corrals. The new
arrangement resulted in bringing thousands more cattle to the Outlet.

As the cattle business stabilized, a

Scenes such as this were typical in the Cherokee Outlet after the Civil War as millions of head of
cattle passed through the Outlet en route to eastern markets. [Courtesy Western History
Collections, University of Oklahoma Library.]

large number of white men acquired legal residence. They built temporary homes for themselves and their employees, including hundreds of cowboys. Life in the Cherokee Outlet seemed ideal.[13]

Unfortunately, the peaceful existence was not to last. Already others were looking longingly at this choice land. These included families moving west-ward seeking a place to homestead, farmers who had failed in other locations, and railroads seeking routes into the Oklahoma Territory.

In 1879, a man appeared almost suddenly on the scene to forge these groups into a unit and to threaten the cattlemen's hold on their Strip ranges.

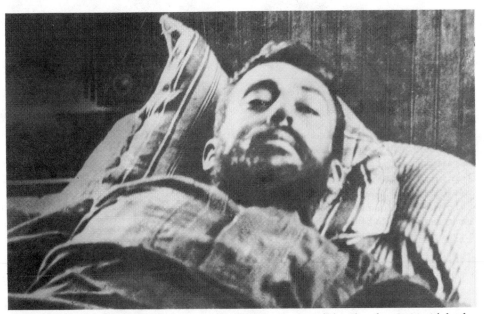

Nathaniel (Zip) Wyatt alias Dick Yeager and his cronies terrorized the Cherokee Strip with bank and train robberies and murders. He was finally wounded and captured by a posse in August 1895 and died in the Garfield County jail in Enid on September 7. [Courtesy Western History Collections, University of Oklahoma Library.]

Elias C. Boudinot, a Cherokee whose father was assassinated for signing the New Echota Treaty in 1835, was a leading agitator for colonizing the Oklahoma lands. He said they had been bought from the Indians, were public lands, and subject to homesteading. [Courtesy Oklahoma Historical Society, neg. #5142.]

Capt. David L. Payne organized the Boomers and led them into the Oklahoma Territory and the Cherokee Strip. [Courtesy Oklahoma Historical Society, neg. #15118.]

This is one of David L. Payne's early excursions into the Oklahoma Territory. In June 1884 he attempted to set up a colony in the Cherokee Outlet. [Courtesy Oklahoma Historical Society, neg. #15574.]

Chapter Four

On to the Cherokee Strip!

1889 Land Rush Stirs Settlers

As SOON AS the Civil War ended in 1865, a wave of immigrants moved onto the western plains. Under the Homestead Act of 1862, any citizen who was head of a family or over 21 years of age and who had been loyal to the government during the war could homestead 160 acres of land in the public domain.

Thousands of easterners, many of them war veterans, took advantage of the offer in Kansas. They settled not only on public lands but many encroached on Indian lands. Their actions resulted in bloody battles between Indians and whites. Pressures grew to open more Indian lands to settlement.

After the Treaties of 1866, many of the land hungry looked to the Indian Territory for future homes. By the treaties, the government purchased large areas from the Creeks and Seminoles. These were now unoccupied except for herds of cattle and were called the Unassigned Lands. Others looked longingly at the Cherokee Outlet, although this was still owned by the Cherokees.

It is little wonder the homesteaders became intensely interested in Indian

Territory lands. Drovers bringing their cattle through the Territory and the Outlet into Kansas brought tales of the breath-taking beauty of the land. They told of acres and acres of luxuriant grass and crystal clear streams. Along the streams were willow, cottonwood, and elm trees, and in some of the lower areas were hackberry, mulberry, walnut, pecan and oak trees. The streams were described as being full of fish, and along the banks were many fur-bearing animals. The fields abounded in quail, wild turkeys, and prairie chickens. Deer and antelope frolicked in the tall prairie grass.[1]

After 1866, a few settlers tried to homestead in the Territory and the Outlet. They were promptly expelled by the army. But 1871 saw the beginning of a more serious effort to open the Oklahoma Territory to settlement.

Settlers Camp in Oklahoma

Elias C. Boudinot, whose father was assassinated after the 1835 Cherokee Treaty of New Echota, had joined the

Katy Railroad with headquarters at Parsons, Kansas. His boss, Robert S. Stevens, was eager to expand the Katy route through the Indian Territory.

In August 1871, writing under the pen name, Montauk, he published in the Lawrence, Kansas, *Tribune* his contention that the Oklahoma Territory was in the public domain and that any person eligible under the Homestead Act had a right to settle there.[2] His argument was simple: the United States had purchased the land from the Indians, and the title was absolute without reservations. The land therefore was in public domain and subject to homesteading.[3]

Milton W. Reynolds, whom Boudinot had met at the Fort Smith Council, was publisher of the *Parsons Sun*. He disagreed with Boudinot. He argued that only Congress had a right to open land to settlement, but he published the Boudinot article and scattered thousands of copies throughout the frontier. The article stirred the settlers and by November 1871 at least 500 were encamped in the Territory. William W. Belknap, Secretary of War, promptly had them expelled. The action, however, had little lasting effect. As soon as soldiers were out of sight, settlers returned. The scene was repeated again and again until 1879. Then Boudinot wrote another article, this time for the *Chicago Times*. He was working in Washington, D.C., possibly still a Katy agent.[3]

He restated even more emphatically his arguments that Oklahoma lands were in the public domain. The article attracted national attention. Once again large numbers of hopeful settlers invaded the Territory. The most publicized

Gathered around this chuck wagon are not cowboys but cattlemen holding a last-minute council to discuss how to prevent the opening of the Cherokee Strip. [Courtesy Kansas State Historical Society.]

actions were those of Charles C. Carpenter, who led a group of settlers into the Territory and defied the government. When soldiers closed in on his encampment, he fled.

The Boomers Organize

Suddenly, in the fall of 1879, the colonization effort took on new life as Capt. David L. Payne, Civil War veteran, Indian fighter, and frontiersman arrived on the scene and began organizing his Oklahoma Colony. Shortly before his arrival, he had been Assistant Doorkeeper of the United States House of Representatives, where he and Boudinot had discussed the Oklahoma question. He, too, had close ties with the railroads.

Payne was 43, tall, broad-shouldered, and persuasive. He was well-versed in homestead laws, and he completely endorsed Boudinot's contention that Oklahoma lands were subject to homesteading. He believed that if he could force the issue before the courts, this view would be upheld. His plan was to establish colonies in the Unassigned Lands.

Thousands of land hungry settlers had moved into southern Kansas by the end of 1879 and Payne had little difficulty recruiting members for his Oklahoma Colony. Dues were two dollars. Among the rewards for membership would be 160 acres in the Oklahoma Territory. Payne's Colony was made up largely of hungry farmers but also included some business people and adventurers. His assortment of frontier people became known as the Boomers.

By the spring of 1880, Payne had recruited about 1,500 members. Small settlements had formed all along the southern Kansas line awaiting a move into the Oklahoma Territory. Payne led

a group of 21 hardy Boomers into the territory on April 26. They were tracked down by army units and arrested on May 15.

Payne Invades the Strip

Payne was disappointed when he was unable to challenge the arrest before a federal court but when he returned he was welcomed as a hero and interest grew in his cause. From then until 1885, the Boomers ventured into the Territory 15 times and each time they were expelled. In June 1884, Payne took action that caused alarm among cattlemen, Indians, and military officers. He set up a Boomer colony in the Cherokee Outlet. The settlement was located about five miles south of Hunnewell, Kansas, on the Chikaskia River. It was called Rock Falls for falls on the nearby river. Within a month, 1,500 settlers had flocked to Rock Falls, and buildings were under construction on a Main street 100 feet wide. There, Payne set up a shop to print *The Oklahoma War Chief,* the Boomers' newspaper.

Payne's invasion of Cherokee land was of special concern because already many intruders had tried to settle there. The army moved quickly to break up the camp in spite of Payne's claim the Strip was in public domain because it was a part of Oklahoma. All of Rock Falls buildings were burned. Many settlers, fearing arrest, left quickly. Payne and several leaders were taken to Fort Smith and held for 32 days.[4]

In November 1884, the Boomers received exciting news. In September, Payne and 10 of his leaders had gone voluntarily before a grand jury in Topeka and testified to their invasions into the Territory. They were immediately indicted and a trial was set for November before federal district Judge Cassius G. Foster. The *Topeka Capital* said, "The decision will virtually settle as to whether the Oklahoma country belongs to the Indians or not."

Judge Foster quashed the indictments and ruled that settling on the lands was not a criminal offense. The Boomers celebrated and proclaimed the Oklahoma lands had at last been opened.[5] Their joy was short-lived as the government ignored the ruling and continued to arrest and expel intruders.

Oklahoma Bill Passes

Payne wearily made plans to begin another invasion but the Boomer efforts had taken their toll on his health. He died while eating breakfast in Wellington on November 27, 1884. His colony vice president, William Lewis Couch, immediately took command. Couch was equally capable, determined, and thoroughly knowledgeable in homestead laws.

Couch immediately organized the Boomers for another invasion of the Territory and his caravan of 200 settlers arrived on Stillwater Creek, just south of

the Cherokee Outlet on December 12. They called their settlement "the town of Stillwater," but they were evicted by the U.S. Cavalry in the spring of 1885.

After another brief invasion in 1885, Couch decided to disband the Boomers. Public opinion was turning in their favor, and great headway was being made in Washington for the Oklahoma cause. Several bills had been introduced to open the Unassigned lands to settlement. Couch and his key aides went to Washington to help press for congressional action.

Victory finally came in 1889. On February 1, the U.S. House of Representatives passed a bill introduced in 1888 by William M. Springer of Illinois. And after bitter opposition from cattlemen, they secured passage in the Senate by making it a rider to the Indian Appropriation Bill. President Grover Cleveland signed the bill on March 3, 1889, making the Unassigned Lands a part of the public domain and open to settlement.

The cattlemen had good reason to oppose the bill, because one article authorized appointment of a commission to negotiate with the Cherokees for the purchase of the Cherokee Outlet and

with other Indians for the purchase of their surplus lands. As the tide turned in favor of the Boomers, it was also turning against the Cherokee Strip Live Stock Association's possession of the Outlet.

The Rush Into Oklahoma

At noon on April 22, 1889, thousands of settlers participated in the great land rush into the Unassigned Lands to claim the 11,000 quarter-sections of the Oklahoma Territory. Before nightfall, scores of new towns were born. Immediately, the settlers set up homes and businesses and most communities established village newspapers.

The land opening stirred homesteaders' interest in the Strip even more. Thousands of them had passed through the land en route to the Unassigned Lands. Scarcely had the dust settled on the run than a clamor began to open the Strip to settlement. From 1879 until 1889, the cry had been "On to Oklahoma!" Now it became "On to the Cherokee Strip!" Railroads, farmers, border towns, and wholesale centers joined newspapers. The tide

to open the Outlet was becoming overwhelming.

Certainly the time was ripe for action. The Live Stock Association's five year lease on the Outlet expired in 1888, and Chief Dennis Bushyhead, who had pushed the lease through the Cherokee National Council in 1883, had not been reelected. His successor, Joel B. Mayes, had refused to approve a renewal. The tribe was divided over the lease. Mayes said other groups were offering more money. One syndicate offered to buy the entire Outlet for $18,000,000.

Finally, in late 1888, the Cherokees approved a new five-year lease with the Association for $200,000 per year, but even this was to no avail. The government, yielding to pressures to open the Outlet to settlement, declared the lease void.

Cattlemen Ordered Out

The bill that had passed in 1889 setting up a commission to negotiate with the Cherokees for the purchase of the Outlet instructed the commission to offer the Cherokees $1.25 per acre for

To make the 1889 Oklahoma land run, thousands of settlers crossed the Cherokee Strip in prairie schooners. In 1893, many decided to run for homesteads in the Strip. [Courtesy *The Stillwater NewsPress.*]

the land. Secretary of the Interior John M. Noble now warned the Cherokees to accept the offer. And President Benjamin Harrison, after an opinion from his Attorney General that the Live Stock Association's lease was without legal force, issued a proclamation forbidding all grazing in the Outlet. He ordered all cattle removed from the Outlet by October 1, 1890.

With the President's proclamation, the Live Stock Association saw its last hopes vanish. Its members were forced to market as many of their cattle as possible and to find ranges elsewhere for those left.

The Cherokees knew, too, they were fighting a losing battle. In 1891, a bill was introduced in Congress to pay the tribe $1.25 an acre for Outlet lands and to take them without further negotiation. The Cherokees feared that if they failed to accept the offer, the Outlet might be taken from them. In late 1891, they ceded the lands to the government for $8,595,750, less than half the amount offered them by the syndicate earlier. This amounted to an estimated $1.29 per acre. The agreement was ratified by Congress and by the Cherokee National Council in March and April 1893.*

The die was now cast. On August 19, 1893, President Cleveland issued a proclamation opening the Outlet and the surplus lands of the Pawnees and Tonkawas for settlement at noon on September 16, 1893. This would bring about the greatest land run in American history. The great rangeland of the Cherokee Strip would be converted to waving fields of wheat.

---

* In 1961, after years of litigation, the Cherokees were awarded an additional $14,789,000 for their Outlet lands. Other judgments totaling nearly $19 million were awarded as aditional payments in 1961 and 1973. (Earl Boyd and Rennard Strickland, *The Cherokee People*, Indian Tribal Series: Phoenix, 1973, pp. 48, 63.)

After their victory in Congress, hopeful settlers gathered for the run into Oklahoma. Scarcely had the dust settled on the 1889 run than their cry became "On to the Cherokee Strip!" [Courtesy Oklahoma Historical Society, neg. #11648.]

Chapter Five

Preparing for the Opening

Rules Are Set for the Strip Run

IT TOOK SEVERAL MONTHS to prepare President Cleveland's proclamation. When it was released on August 19, 1893, it was 15,000 words in length. It dealt in great detail with every facet of the Strip opening. The *Perkins Bee*, a small Payne County weekly, printed all of the proclamation and it filled nearly an entire page in very small type.[1]

The President set Saturday, September 16 at noon as the starting time for the run. Most of the land to be opened was that controlled by the Cherokee Strip Live Stock Association from 1883 to 1888. This was approximately 200 miles from east to west and about 58 miles from north to south.

On October 21, 1891 the Tonkawa Indians ceded their reservation to the United States. Members of the tribe were given individual land allotments and the tribe was paid $30,600 as further compensation for relinquishment of their rights. In November 1892, the Pawnees had ceded all of their land to the government for $80,000. The Pawnees, also, were given individual allotments. The remainder of the Tonkawa and Pawnee

reservations became public domain and were to be opened to settlement the same as other areas of the Strip.[2]

This meant that approximately 6,500,000 acres would be available for homesteading, less about 760,000 acres set aside for schools, public buildings, and county seats. The Strip's total area was greater than that of any of several states, including Massachusetts, New Hampshire, Vermont, or New Jersey.[3]

While these figures are impressive, not nearly enough land was available to provide 160 acres for each of the thousands gathering for the run. Many would turn wearily homeward afterward, but each seemed to feel he would not be among the unfortunate.

Nine Booths Set Up

The government decided to permit the land rush only from the north and south borders of the Strip. Nine booths were to be set up for home-seekers to register for the run. These were at Stillwater, Orlando, Hennessey, and Goodwin (south of Woodward), Oklahoma, and on the north border at Kiowa, Cameron, Hunnewell, Caldwell, and Arkansas City, Kansas.[4]

Congress had empowered the Secretary of the Interior to divide the Strip into counties. The President's proclamation thus set boundaries for seven counties it designated by the letters K, L, M, N, O, P, and Q. These would later become Kay, Grant, Woods, Woodward, Garfield, Noble, and Pawnee counties.[5] This was a carryover from earlier land openings in which letters A through H were used to designate counties.[6]

Townsites for county seats were laid out in each county and four acres in each one were reserved for a courthouse. Sec-

retary of the Interior Hoke Smith admired the small towns centered around public squares in his native Georgia and he ordered county seats in the Cherokee Strip patterned after them. This is why all of the original county seat business districts except Woodward are on squares surrounding the courthouses. County seats were to have eight-foot sidewalks and streets 80 feet wide. Sections 16 and 36 of every township were reserved for public schools. Other sections were reserved for university, agricultural college, and other such purposes.

The government established seven townsites, each containing 320 acres. These were at what later became Perry,

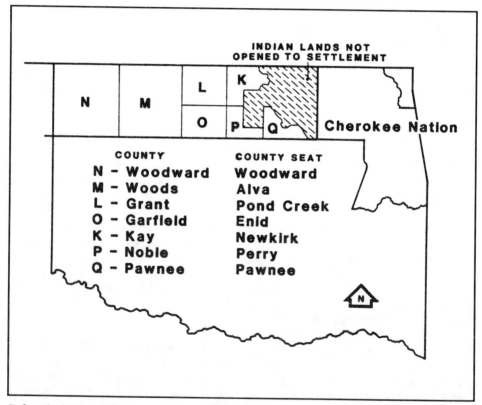

COUNTY	COUNTY SEAT
N – Woodward	Woodward
M – Woods	Alva
L – Grant	Pond Creek
O – Garfield	Enid
K – Kay	Newkirk
P – Noble	Perry
Q – Pawnee	Pawnee

Before the land run, the government used letters of the alphabet to designate counties to be settled and laid out townsites for county seats. In the November 1984 general election, voters chose names for counties. [Map by Mike Shores, Assistant Planner, City of Stillwater.]

Pawnee, Alva, Enid, Pond Creek, Newkirk, and Woodward. Land offices were set up in the Enid, Alva, Woodward, and Perry districts for home-seekers to file their claims after the run.[7]

Sooners Sneak In

Secretary Smith designed a system which he hoped would thwart Sooners who flocked to the land runs. It was estimated that 2,000 of them were already scattered on the Strip borders by September 1, 1893.[8] One writer of that day described them thus:

Now the sooner is looked upon as a thief. He steals across the line before the opening and hides in the brush or ravine and squats on the claim just about the time or a few minutes after the opening hour. The honest home-seeker may make a twelve or fifteen mile run for that particular quarter and when he gets there finds a sooner has been sitting there for an hour.[9]

Smith ordered a 100-foot "neutral zone" around the Strip. Inside these would be the registration booths. Each homesteader would have to register and sign a form stating he was eligible to make the run. He would later have to sign an affidavit at the land office that he had not entered the Strip ahead of the signal. The plan was cheered at first, as most of the eligible homesteaders despised the Sooners. When the plan turned out later to be an utter failure, both it and Smith were ridiculed.

A dispute arose as to whether settlers could make the run by train. Smith ruled that trains could be used but they could travel only 15 miles per hour and stop at points not more than five miles

Even as preparations were being made for the land run, hopeful homesteaders began gathering at Walnut River near Arkansas City. These were some early arrivals. [Courtesy Kansas State Historical Society.]

apart.[10] The purpose of this was to prevent trains from outrunning other vehicles and horses and giving train riders an advantage.

Rules for the Strip run contained a provision that made it different from the other land runs. This land would not be free. Each settler would have to pay for his claim. The government wanted to recover some of the more than $850,000,000. it paid to the Cherokees. It arbitrarily decided that some sections of the Strip were worth more than others. Homesteaders would have to pay $2.50 per acre for lands in the eastern section, $1.50 per acre for those in the central section, and $1.00 per acre for those in the west.

The eastern dividing line would be along the western boundaries of present-day Kay and Noble counties. The central-western line would be the eastern border of present Woods county. The charge failed to deter eager settlers. Most never paid for their land as Congress nullified the payments in May 1900.

Sheriffs and Judges Chosen

As the date of the run grew near, the government took steps which it hoped would prevent some of the hardships settlers endured during earlier land runs. Col. Alfred P. Swineford, a representative of the General Land Office, awarded contracts to dig large water wells in each of the new townsites. The wells were to be completed by September 16, and Swineford predicted they would "furnish ample water supply for every man and beast entering the new territory."[11]

Swineford also took steps to assure law and order. The bill providing for the

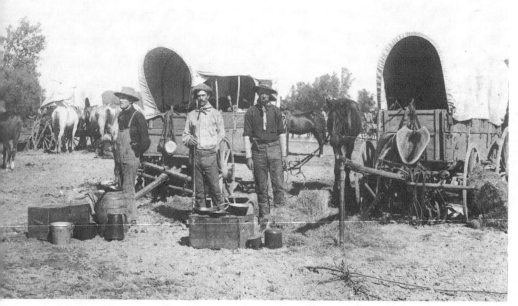

Wooden boxes, barrels, buckets, shovels, and a supply of hay were the staples on prairie schooners getting ready for the Cherokee Strip land run. The ground was barren and dusty. [Courtesy Kansas State Historical Society.]

Strip opening also provided it would become a part of the Oklahoma Territory immediately, and the settlers would be governed by the laws of the Territory. Swineford selected sheriffs and probate judges for each of the new counties and said they would be on duty from the opening day.[12]

To help assure a food supply, 20 ex-packing house butchers from Chicago arrived by train on September 9 in Arkansas City. They brought one car filled with horses to ride during the land run and 35 tents. Their aim was to scatter into the new towns and have butcher shops operating within a day or two.[13]

With all these preparations, the government seemed ready for the great day ahead, and tension was growing by the minute among the thousands dreaming of success in a momentous historic event.

On the day of the Cherokee Strip land run, scores of citizens arrived on a cattle car traveling from Anthony, Kansas, to Cameron, the site of a registration booth. [Courtesy Kansas State Historical Society.]

TOP: Registration lines at Arkansas City were sometimes a mile long with four abreast. Many collapsed from heat and thirst. [Courtesy Kansas State Historical Society.]
BOTTOM: Thousands of home-seekers gathered at booths like these along the north and south borders of the Cherokee Strip to register in advance for the 1893 land run. The government thought the system would thwart Sooners trying to sneak in early. [Courtesy H. E. Ricker Family.]

Chapter Six

The Grand Opening

A Day of Triumph and Tragedy

AS SOON AS President Cleveland issued the proclamation opening the Cherokee Strip to settlement, a wave of excitement swept over the western frontier and to all parts of the nation.

The Guthrie (Okla.) *Daily News* was named official publication for the proclamation and it immediately published thousands of copies. More than 2,500 were sold on the first day. Orders poured in via telegraph from throughout the nation. A thousand were sold in Oklahoma City, and hundreds were distributed along the towns bordering the Strip both in Kansas and Oklahoma.[1]

Reporters flocked to the area. The Strip opening was big news and they seized upon any incident for a story. Often their information was wrong. Most reported trains could be used to make the run.[2] Secretary of the Interior Hoke Smith had not announced the approval of trains and the erroneous news items caused thousands of settlers to come pouring into southern Kansas by train.

Almost by magic, caravans of prairie schooners appeared on roads leading to the Strip border. Adorning the sides of most schooners were slogans, the most frequent of which were "Oklahoma or Bust" and "In God We Trust."[3]

Drought Brings Suffering

Most of the occupants of the wagons and the horses that pulled them were gaunt from lack of water and food. In the 1893 summer, the Kansas-Oklahoma area suffered from one of its worst droughts. No rain had fallen in August. The sun beat down unmercifully on the travelers, causing daily temperatures of more than 100 degrees.

An eyewitness to the scene was nine-year old Clyde E. Muchmore. He lived in the small town of Kiowa, which had been designated the site of a registration booth. In August 1893 Clyde accompanied his father and a family friend on a wagon trip along the Strip border and into the Strip for several miles, hopeful of finding a suitable claim site before the run. Years later he became publisher of the Ponca City, Oklahoma, *News,* a leading newspaper of the Strip. He recorded his memories of the events:

> Not during the whole trip..do we recall seeing a single cloud that suggested rain.Daily the sun beat down, drying up creek and spring and parching vegetation...man and beast found it difficult to make watering places in a day's drive...there were tales from much suffering from lack of water. The heat was too intense to make that kind of travel pleasant and the horses showed the effect of rough trails, short water rations and parched grass for food.[4]

As homesteaders neared the Strip border, conditions became even worse. Clouds of dust stirred by the hot winds were mixed with black clouds of ash from grassland burned by soldiers. On August 9, General John M. Schofield had ordered military troops to remove all unauthorized persons from the Strip. Four troops of cavalry from Fort Reno and Fort Supply and four more from Fort Riley, Kansas, were assigned to the task.

Rumors were rife that many Sooners were already in the Strip, hiding in gullies, behind rocks, and in the tall prairie grass. Kansas cattlemen were also slipping across the border, grazing their cattle on the Strip grass and making stacks of hay.

The soldiers set fire to grass all along the Strip border and burned hay stacks. Their method ended the problem of intruding cattlemen and flushed out a few Sooners, but it also created more heat and clouds of smoke that made the camping areas even more stifling.

Stillwater, Oklahoma, founded during the run of 1889, lost about half of its population during the 1893 Cherokee Strip run. Many were in this line which was estimated to be about three-fourths of a mile long. [Courtesy H. E. Ricker Family.]

Thousands Gather

In spite of the heat, lack of water, and other problems, the settlers kept pouring in. Estimates by those present at the time vary widely, but as the influx grew, from 10,000 to 15,000 were reported camped around the small village of Kiowa, whose normal population was 700. Another gathering of 15,000 was reported at Caldwell further east.[5]

On the Strip's southern border, from 15,000 to 25,000 gathered at Orlando, one of the first small communities settled during the Oklahoma run of 1889. Many of the settlers who came south then were ready now to rush north into the Strip. Thousands more gathered at Stillwater, about 20 miles east of Orlando.[6]

All of these were dwarfed by the huge masses that poured into Arkansas City, which had promoted itself as the ideal place to camp and to make the run for a choice claim. Its success was phenomenal. Otis Lorton, who later became a writer for the *Tulsa Daily World,* was present and recorded that "Arkansas City's population of 4,500 was swollen until it held 70,000 people, most of them hoping, praying, fighting for home in the new land." And Lorton described the scene:

In the throng were men and women from all walks of life, artists out from the east to get "color," writers, lawyers, doctors, gamblers galore, down-and-outers looking for a chance to make some easy money—rich man, poor man, beggar man, thief—but most of all the family man who wanted a home. They were all armed, many desperate, and it was a mighty tough crowd in spots.[7]

The grass apparently looked greener on the other side of the fence to these settlers who gathered near Arkansas City. Actually most of the grass in the Strip had been scorched to death by the blistering sun or by soldiers trying to flush out Sooners. [Courtesy Kansas State Historical Society.]

Many Are Destitute

Some hopeful settlers came to escape dire circumstances they faced back home. Many banks in the nation closed in 1893 and jobs were hard to find. The Strip offered hope of a new beginning. Approximately 40,000 homesteads would be available during the run and it was certain that thousands of people would be disappointed. Yet, each believed someone else would be among the unfortunate.

Life came to a standstill in many towns near the Strip because hired help was not available. Livery stable employees, farm workers, domestic help, school teachers, and servants all headed for the Strip. Some women felt that a homestead would be a good lure for capturing a husband. A Guthrie newspaper reported

that many of its Black population were preparing for the run.[8]

As they arrived on the Strip border, settlers quickly positioned their wagons on the line for the run, then set up camp further back.

By early September, the Strip border was almost one vast encampment. Living conditions were barely tolerable. Water was two miles away. Many home-seekers had meager food supplies and little money. Toilet facilities were primitive. The sun and dust continued to bear down unmercifully.

Boarding houses in Strip towns helped alleviate hunger by delivering food to the camps. Church groups raised money to provide water to some of the suffering. Peddlers sold sandwiches, hard boiled eggs, and bread to those who could afford them.[9] In some areas ven-

As the day of the run neared, frustration grew and tempers flared. Many settlers carried guns. These were in Harper County, Kansas, just north of Grant County, Oklahoma. [Courtesy Kansas State Historical Society.]

dors sold water for one dollar per bucket.[10]

Fast Horses Arrive

At night, by the light of fires or lanterns, the settlers discussed their hopes and fears. On maps of the Strip, they pinpointed choice homestead sites and discussed how to claim them first. Their fears centered around trains and horses. Would the trains outrun their wagons to the best claims? Could those in wagons compete against the many race horses being imported?

On both the northern and southern borders of the Strip, train loads of horses and ponies were arriving from Colorado, Texas, and even Oregon. They were bought up quickly. Rumors spread that Sooners or those with fast horses might rush into the Strip and blow up railroad bridges. As the day of the run neared, most men in the camps were wearing guns.[11]

Adding to the confusion was an influx of confidence men and gamblers. The streets and camps were full of them. Many settlers were fleeced out of their money, food, and even their horses.[12]

Each day tension had increased along the Strip, and on Saturday, September 9, the situation could be described only as a frenzy. Registration booths were to be open from 7 a.m. to 6 p.m. starting the following Monday. They would remain open until September 16. By this time at least 100,000 home-seekers were jammed in the registration areas and more were still flocking in. Fearful of not getting registered on time, they began standing in line a full week before the run on Saturday, September 16.

For a week preceding the land run, riders rode along the lines of settlers, keeping order and reviving those who collapsed from lack of food or water. [Courtesy OSU Library, Special Collections.]

By Sunday afternoon, lines stretched almost as far as the eye could see at some booths. B. L. Long, who settled in Ponca City, recalled the scene at Arkansas City:

> The line had soon grown to four and five deep and a mile long...We were in that line from Sunday morning until three o'clock Wednesday evening, and we did not leave it night or day for fear of losing our places. By turns, one of us would carry food and drink to the others.[13]

Lines of Death

Forty-five clerks had been assigned to handle registration at the booths. The government had added a booth at Guthrie, Oklahoma, to speed up registration, and after the first day ordered the Arkansas City booth open 24 hours a day.

The folly and tragedy of Secretary of the Interior Smith's plan became more evident by the minute. The searing heat and dust caused indescribable suffering. Under a heading, "Lines of Death," an Arkansas City newspaper reported that more than 50 were overcome by heat in one day, six of whom died before night. Twenty more collapsed at Caldwell, and 22 at Orlando. After suffering from daytime heat, the settlers often became cold at night as temperatures dropped drastically.[14]

Covered wagons began pulling into position as the hour of the Strip run neared. [Courtesy Archives and Manuscripts Division, Oklahoma Historical Society, neg. #10605.]

Judge Preston Gillett made the run from Hennessey and recalled:

Large numbers perished from the lack of water mostly...Water sold for five cents a glass and those that did not have the five cents went without. Many old people and those sick or disabled found graves instead of homes. I think I spent $5.00 for water.[15]

In spite of suffering and tragedies, the homesteaders clung to their dream and stayed in lines. They justified the description of a Cherokee Strip Guide reporter:

The home-seekers on the border are not of the boom class, but a sturdy, intelligent, typically American element...They go in advance of everything, bold, fearless, ever progressing, undaunted, unterrified...[16]

By Friday, September 15, the eve of the run, thousands had obtained registration slips, but it was estimated that as many as 20,000 were still frantically trying to register at Arkansas City. Extra clerks were added and worked all night at the booths to process them.[17]

Ready and Set

The past four weeks had seemed like an eternity to many, but at last the fateful day arrived. Saturday, September 16, came—dry, dusty, and with a blazing sun. Suspense gripped the encampments as settlers lined up for the race. As noon neared, as far as the eye could see was a black, swaying line of vehicles, horses, and human beings. Every conceivable conveyance was there—wagons, carts, buggies, thoroughbred race horses, cow

The Strip land run is only minutes away as the flag man rides out and positions himself for starting the run. [Courtesy Kansas State Historical Society.]

ponies, and even bicycles.[18] Several hundred women were among the masses, most of them driving one-horse or two-horse vehicles, but some were astride race horses or atop the trains.

Soldiers with carbine rifle were stationed every 600 yards waiting to give the starting signal at exactly noon and to halt anyone who broke the line ahead of time. The latter effort caused great frustration and even tragedy.

A deaf man thought the signal had been given and his horse moved forward. He was shot from the saddle by a patrolling soldier. As a shot was heard in the distance, a man on a thoroughbred horse took off. He was shot in the head by a drunken soldier when he refused to stop.[19]

A line south of the Chilocco Indian school reservation charged into the Strip eight minutes early after a soldier accidentally discharged his rifle. The nervous settlers jumped the gun a minute before noon near Hunnewell. At Orlando, a wild shot sent thousands on their way three minutes ahead of schedule. As many as 11,000 started early at Hennessey.

And at Last, Go!

When noon at last came, shots were fired officially all along the Strip. The greatest race in world history began as from 100,000 to 150,000 surged forward. With them went the trains, notably the Rock Island with its 42 passenger cars, its whistle blowing, its bells ringing, and passengers cheering.

Within seconds a thick cloud of dust and ashes arose over the area and within two minutes the homesteaders were almost out of sight. Taking the lead in the

Now, only seconds remain before the noon signal. The wagons, buggies, and horsemen are lined up for miles. The long-awaited dream is almost a reality. [Courtesy Kansas State Historical Society.]

rush were men on horseback. Light carts were close behind. Then came buckboards, buggies, spring wagons, and farm wagons.

There were almost as many stories about the run as there were participants. One man, seeing a woman behind him on the same piece of land, left it for her to claim. After he was out of sight, the claimant quickly took off some of "her" attire, and it was a man.[20] A blind man stepped across the line to file acclaim but was lost in the dust cloud. A settler from Kiowa rode one horse and led three others behind him, switching horses as one tired. Sooners were blamed for setting fires near choice claims to keep others out.

Horses broke their legs stepping into holes, some men broke their legs jumping from trains. The landscape was strewn with stoves, buckets, feed boxes, and bales of hay. Now and then a shout echoed, "Sooner! Sooner! Shoot the S.O.B." And shots rang out.[21]

"Cow Horses" Win

Before the race had gone a mile in the blinding dust, settlers riding ordinary "cow horses" had the last laugh over those who had imported expensive race

Almost every account of the Cherokee Strip land run has included this photograph credited to W. S. Prettyman. Some historians believe Prettyman set up a platform for taking pictures and then participated in the run, leaving his helpers to do the actual shooting. [Courtesy Oklahoma Historical Society, neg. #10601.]

horses. Preston Gillett was one of 13,000 settlers jammed into 46 cattle cars on a train that took off from Hennessey at the sound of the gun. His brother, Guy, was riding a farm horse for which he had agreed to pay $60 if he won a claim and $5 if he lost.[22]

Preston watched from the train and saw race horses drop dead in their tracks, prodded unmercifully by inexperienced horsemen. Guy forged ahead and claimed one of the best lots in Enid for himself and another for Preston. The latter jumped from the train before it stopped and staked claim to his lot just ahead of the mass of humanity that came swarm-ing from the train. At Kiowa, Kansas, a buckskin pony also proved superior, out-running a Kentucky-bred race horse to a lot in Alva.

Council G. Crawford narrowly es-caped death in his race. After he had traveled about six miles, he and other riders were ordered to stop by a drunken soldier looking for Sooners. As the riders swept past him, the soldier fired and shot a man near Crawford from his saddle. After a 16-mile ride in a hour and 10 minutes, Crawford staked his claim near Ponca City.[23]

Tom Grodonovitch, a native of Yugo-slavia, could not speak English. He car-

John Noble made the great land run and later did this historic painting, "The Run." The original color art is now on a 7-by-8-foot canvass at the Woolaroc Museum near Bartlesville. [Courtesy Woolaroc Museum.]

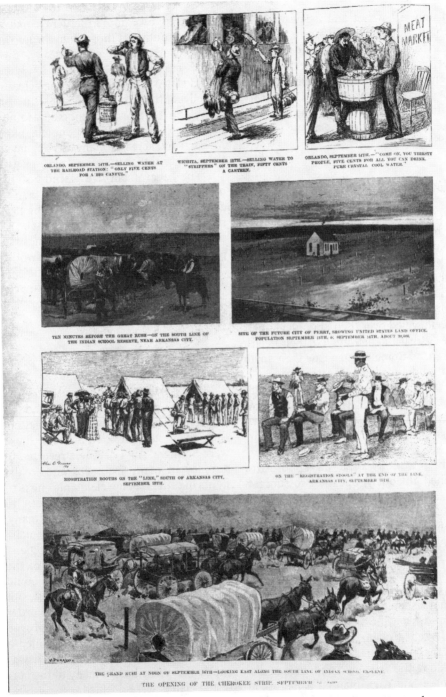

Harper's Weekly told the Cherokee Strip run story with these drawings. Top cartoons show water being sold to thirsty homesteaders, and the bottom drawing is another version of the run. The second panel shows Perry land office just before 20,000 people stampeded there. [Courtesy Kansas State Historical Society.]

ried only a hatchet and a few items of clothing. But he climbed atop a train and clung tenaciously with both hands as hopefuls crowded each other for space. When the train slowed to five miles per hour north of present day Ponca City, Grodonovitch jumped from the train, and staked a claim by digging a hole with his hatchet.[24]

Some Women Succeed

Only a few women sought to endure the hardships of the Strip run. Their suffering was great but some triumphed. Writers often bemoaned the conditions of the women..."their faces black with tears and dirt, their eyes red and in many instances almost blind, their hair hanging disheveled over their shoulders, their dresses torn and bedraggled, their health broken."[25] Some women saw their small children die for lack of water.

Yet some succeeded in their land quest. One woman raced from the line at Arkansas City in a two-wheeled cart. Clinging to her on the back of the cart was her elderly mother-in-law. The cart bobbed and swayed as spectators watched anxiously, but the two successfully staked claims.[26] One woman was burned to death in the high prairie grass set afire by the Sooners.

Another—a widow seeking a new start in life—sat on the tail-board of a wagon driven by her son. Each was seeking a claim. Shortly after the race started, the horses bolted and the woman was bounced from the wagon. Unperturbed, she staked a claim where she fell and lived there for years.[27]

Along the way, men and women dismounted and each planted a flag. Said one observer, "They dropped so quick, it was like rain drops from clouds. They were here, there, and everywhere."

Within two hours, settlers coming from the south met those from the north. The great run was over. Ideally, this would be the point at which a writer would state, "They all found homesteads and lived happily ever after." But for many, the fight for a new home was only beginning. Instead of just one claimant for each 160 acres, as many as 10 claimed to be first on the site.

The government had placed a stone marker with a legal description on the corner of each quarter section. The first settler to arrive was to drive a stake in the ground, hopefully with a witness to prove he was the first claimant. He would then go to the land office and file his claim. Eventually, each would appear personally before land office officials and "prove up" his claim.[28]

Fighting Erupts

The system did not work out as neatly as hoped. Settlers swarmed on different areas of each quarter section, each claiming to be first. Some of these were Sooners. Angry settlers resorted to gunplay in many instances and to fist fights in others. Some claimants chose to settle the argument by selling out to others from $100 to $300. And many, disillusioned by the dry, dusty plain, packed up and left without a struggle.

It took years to settle some of the claims. The land office officials could decide on which claimant was first, but the Secretary of the Interior could order a re-hearing. If the Secretary approved the land office decision, a title called a patent was issued to the owner. It was nearly five years before many of the contested claims were decided.

As twilight came on September 16, 1893, groups of weary settlers, losers in the great land run, plodded back toward the lines from which they had started at noon. Dejected and disillusioned, they would have to build a life elsewhere.

Those who retraced their path through Arkansas City found the Strip border villages almost deserted. Streets were empty as were many homes. The smell of ashes permeated the air as camp fires still smoldered. But as life seemed to have gone out in southern Kansas, it sprang anew all through the Strip, as the winners in the race overnight began building new homes and new cities.

As soon as the dust settled after the run, sod houses sprang up all across the Cherokee Strip plains. D. G. and Zada Harned built this one near Helena, which was first in Woods and later in Alfalfa County. He is at far right. [Courtesy Edith and Glenn Douglas.]

TOP: A sturdy board walk helped citizens get around the Alva square in the early days. In the background are two historic buildings on the east side, the elegant Runnymede Hotel and the H. M. Bickel building. [Courtesy Alva Centennial Commission.]

BOTTOM: Carry Nation came to Alva periodically from Kiowa, Kansas, with pocketfuls of rocks which she threw at saloons located on the north side of the Alva square. [Courtesy Alva Centennial Commission.]

Chapter Seven

Alva

The Vast "Empire of Woods" Is Settled

As THE SANTA FE RAILROAD network spread over Kansas in 1884, the village of Kiowa sprang up near the southern border. By the late 1880s it had become an important shipping center for cattlemen with herds in the Cherokee Strip. In 1893, Kiowa tried to prepare for its greatest historical moment when the government decided to locate a registration booth there and to make it a jumping-off site for the Cherokee Strip run.

Kiowa's normal population had reached 700, but in September 1893, an estimated 15,000 land-hungry settlers swarmed into the area. Tremendous suffering occurred as the small village was unable to supply water, food, or sanitary facilities for the vast settlement. Gambling, drinking and violence were virtually uncontrolled.

Those who gathered at Kiowa dreamed of a new start in "M" County, an area so vast that it later became know as the "Empire of Woods." It was 48 miles wide and 58 miles from north to south. The goal of many was Alva, the designated county seat, named for Alva Adams, a Santa Fe railroad attorney who later became governor of Colorado. Others wanted a chance to farm the rich wheat-lands.

A few individuals were already on the Alva townsite before the run. Captain F. R. Hardee and 50 cavalrymen were sent from Kiowa to keep order. W. H. Wiggins built land offices at both Woodward and Alva and remained at the latter site. Alva's post office had been established on August 25, 1893. S. L. Johnson, the first postmaster, went to the townsite to prepare for the operation. L. H. Taylor represented the Santa Fe railroad.

Race Horses Collapse

As noon approached, the Kiowa scene closely resembled that at Arkansas City. The temperature was nearing 110 degrees. A cloud of dust hung over the line, mixed with ashes from grass burned by soldiers looking for Sooners. In the line were farmers, laborers, ministers, prospectors, gamblers, lawyers, and even ex-convicts.

Behind the line was a Santa Fe train

ready to wind through Capron, Alva, and Waynoka, dropping settlers along the way. Many clung to the sides, roof, and even the caboose of the train as they awaited the signal for the run to begin. As many as 400 homesteaders lined up at the village of Hardtner, nine miles west of Kiowa, which placed them only 16 miles north of Alva. The race from Kiowa would be about 23 miles.

When noon came on Saturday, September 16, the waiting settlers heard not only the crack of rifle fire, but the blast of a bugle. The race was on, but some never got far. One team of horses broke loose from the wagon and went into the Strip without their owner. Fifty feet across the line, the wheels came off a

wagon and the owner staked a claim there.

E.C. (Evalyn) Aldrich from Chambersville, Mo., charged across the line on a cow pony. After a mile and a half, he paused to count 40 race horses that had collapsed and died from heat, thirst, and over-exertion. Aldrich saw two men with pistols ready to duel over a claim. He stopped and persuaded them to flip a coin instead of kill. Aldrich finished his 26-mile run to a rural claim in two hours.

Stephen B. Tanner may have set a record that day. Having been once a part of the Boomer movement under William L. Couch, Tanner made the first Oklahoma land run in 1889. In 1892, he made the Cheyenne-Arapaho land run. He was

J. W. Montfort's drug store carried a range of merchandise from drugs to paint, wallpaper, and sporting goods. Established in 1894, it anchored the west side of the square. It was later replaced by a brick store that was destroyed by fire on May 22, 1953. [Courtesy Alva Centennial Commission.]

successful a third time as he found a claim during the Strip run. Four of his sons established the Tanner Bros. Mercantile store on the south side of the Alva square.

William Webb of Wellington, Kansas, and some of his family and friends decided they wanted to stick together in the new land. The group of 10 that ran together were his sons, George and Ed, Sam and Phil Paya, Dias Gadbois, Sherman and Roll Dennison, Sam Huff, Barney Carr and Jim Lucus. They followed the railroad track until they passed Capron, then filed claims a half mile apart.

W. W. Wilkinson and his wife, Eve, wanted to keep their six sons and six daughters nearby. They staked a claim northeast of Alva. Their children followed and the family soon owned 1,600 acres in one area. Wilkinson later operated the Farmers Elevator in Alva.

Bickel, Schaeffer Arrive

Others arrived on the Alva townsite that day who were to play important roles in the town's future. Among these were H.M. Bickel, Anton Schaeffer, and Zachariah Boatman. A native of Newark, Ohio, Bickel came from Larned, Kansas. He was a lawyer, but he and his son, Travis, built and operated a meal and flour mill. He brought the first linotype machine to Alva, and his building on the east side of the square was used as a

William A. and Amanda Chick built the St. Nicholas Hotel in 1902 and 1903. The horse-drawn carriage at left brought people from the train station. An Indian in native costume served as bell boy. [Courtesy Alva Centennial Commission.]

typesetting operation for village newspapers.

Schaeffer, later known as Tony Shafer, came to America from Germany in 1873. By the time he was 33, he had gained experience in saddle and harness making in Montana, Colorado, and Kansas. When he made the run into Alva he set up a business on the south side of the square next to Tanner Bros. He later became president of the Alva Bank of Commerce. A cattleman in Texas for many years, Boatman had already spent considerable time in the Strip. After making the run and settling near Alva, he became a real estate broker.

It was still early afternoon as the first riders charged into Alva. L.H. Taylor recorded that the first to arrive was Al Galbraith of Hazelton, Kansas. Just behind him were H.C. McGrath, H.H. Gentry, and Gran Gardner of Deerhead, Kansas.

Following these came waves of other riders and prairie schooners. The train cam puffing in 20 minutes later. By 3 p.m. the townsite was teeming with homesteaders and by nightfall nearly all choice lots had been taken. More than two thousand were milling around by late evening. Perhaps the miracle of the Alva

The frame Alva land office, built before the run by W. H. Wiggins, had an interior considered elegant for 1893. [Courtesy Kansas State Historical Society.]

townsite run was that no serious injuries were reported.

Alva Grows Quickly

The new residents moved quickly to get their town established. By nightfall tents sprang up around the square and on residential lots. Farmers arrived driving wagons carrying barrels of water which they sold by the bucket. Andy Beegle sold lemonade that he brought while making the run. Several snack bars operated from prairie schooners.

These were all makeshift operations.

Building supplies came pouring in by train and wagon, and frame buildings soon replaced tents. Some homes and buildings in Kansas towns were taken apart, hauled to Alva and reassembled. By November, Alva boasted 113 business houses, including several two-story structures.

Religion was a vital part of pioneer life. One the morning after the run, the Reverend F.P. Semands, a Baptist minister from Kiowa, preached a sermon on the square from the back of a wagon. A Union Church building was completed in time for Thanksgiving services.

Individual denominations began to

Temple Houston came to Alva from Woodward to dedicate "The Castle on the Hill" on July 1, 1898. This was the beginning of Northwestern State Normal School, which is now Northwestern Oklahoma State University. The Castle was destroyed by fire in March 1935. [Courtesy Alva Centennial Commission.]

organize soon after that. The Methodists met first in Andy Beegle's cafe on the south side of the square. When Beegle wanted to communicate with Methodists, he stood in front of his cafe and blew his bugle. They gathered to get the word. He was the first Methodist Sunday School superintendent.

"The Castle" is Built

Alva's schools formally began on April 9, 1894 with a three-months term in the Union Church building. Several frame buildings were later used until the first brick school was built in December 1894. The new town had a newspaper from the very first day as W.F. Hatfield printed the *Alva Pioneer* in Hazelton, Kansas, and brought copies with him as he made the run. Among other early newspapers were the *Alva Review*, started in 1894 by Clark Hudson, a populist, and the *Alva Courier*, established in 1896 by A.J. Ross.

The village was incorporated on April 16, 1894, and the county officially became Woods County in the general election of November 1894. It was named for Sam N. Wood, a Kansas territorial legislator and anti-slavery activist. The

In 1910 Alva paved the square and College Avenue. In the background is "The Castle on the Hill." [Courtesy Mary W. Erskine.]

"s" was added in error while the ballots were being prepared.

Alva received a great boost in 1897 when the territorial legislature voted to establish Northwestern State Normal School there. The first building, "The Castle on the Hill," was erected in 1898. Woods was such a vast county that citizens argued over where the courthouse ought to be located. It was finally built on the square at Alva in 1904.

Shortly after that, the "Empire of Woods" would be broken up into several counties, but with all the progress it had made within a few years, Alva was already on its way to becoming a great agricultural hub and the leading educational center of northwestern Oklahoma.

ABOVE: Well-known Alva pioneers operated these stores on the south side of the square in 1909. Sandwiched between Anton Shafer's Harness and Saddlery and F. W. Hanford Hardware, was Tanner Bros. Dry Goods Store. [Courtesy Alva Centennial Commission.]

After operating in a one-story frame building since 1903, Alva officials moved into their new brick city hall in 1911. [Courtesy Alva Centennial Commission.]

After the 1893 land run, Woods County officials transacted business in buildings around the Alva square until this courthouse was built in 1904. [Courtesy Alva Centennial Commission.]

va Roller Mills,
Alva, Okla.

Alva's largest industry was the Alva Roller Mills. The company once had 23 elevators in northwestern communities. Its principal flour brand was Honey Bee. It operated from 1900 until 1958, just south of the Santa Fe depot. [Courtesy Alva Centennial Commission.]

Alva built this opera house in 1907 on Flynn Street to replace an earlier frame building on Barnes Avenue. It featured vaudeville and other live entertainment. It was destroyed by fire on June 22, 1933. [Courtesy Mary W. Erskine.]

Capron was the first townsite on the A.T.&S.F. Railroad when in 1886 it came south from Kiowa, Kansas, into what is now Woods County. Many settlers rushed there and thought it would become a major trade center. It was earlier known as Sterling, Virgel, and Warren. [Courtesy Mary W. Erskine.]

Colonel Andrew Jackson
Blackwell promised that his
"Blackwell Rock" would
endure forever. From an
1894 drawing in the
Blackwell *Times*.]

On Monday, February 28, 1898, Blackwell citizens celebrated the arrival of the H.&S. Railroad.
Famous photographer W. S. Prettyman took this picture. His studio was in the two-story
building. He was mayor from April 1901 to April 1904. [Courtesy of the Oklahoma Historical
Society, neg. #8920.]

Chapter Eight

Blackwell

"The Rock" Endures After 100 Years

THE SETTLING of Blackwell was in several ways similar to that of Ponca City. A group of citizens laid out the townsite before the land run. One man was the driving force in getting the town located and settled, and a fight came about with another village to see which would survive. Blackwell was different in one respect—the town changed names three times within two years.

Shortly after President Grover Cleveland issued the proclamation on August 19, 1893, for opening the Strip to settlement, a group of businessmen from Winfield, Kansas, met and made plans for a new Cherokee Strip town to be called Blackwell Rock. They incorporated under Kansas laws and called themselves The Cherokee Strip Business Exchange and Protective Association.

With this action, Col. Andrew Jackson Blackwell assumed leadership in the movement to establish the new town. Blackwell was born in Gilmore County, Georgia, in 1842. Orphaned and left homeless at age seven, he worked on a farm for his board and clothes until he was 13. He had little schooling.

At age 14, Blackwell moved to Arkansas with a farmer with whom he had lived in Georgia. After five more years of farming, he set out to seek his own fortune and traveled through many parts of the United States. He then returned to Arkansas and over a period of several years amassed a fortune of $40,000 in the mercantile business at Fayetteville.

An adventurer and speculator, Blackwell wanted to be richer. He invested most of his money in bonds and lost all but $2,500. Undaunted, he moved to Joplin, Missouri, entered business again, made a small fortune, and built an opera house. A fire destroyed the opera house and Blackwell found himself broke again.

He Secures a Townsite

Still determined to make a fortune, Blackwell arrived in the Cherokee Nation in 1886, afoot and without even a change of clothes. He was now 44. Once again, his efforts bore fruit. Within four years he had acquired 3,500 acres of land on

Prios Creek near Chelsea in the Indian Territory. And in another two years he had acquired 200 more acres along the Grand River.

A part of the land acquisition came through his marriage to Rosa Vaught, a mixed-blood Cherokee who had allotments near Chelsea. Blackwell and Rosa were wed shortly after he arrived in the Cherokee Nation. They had two sons. Blackwell, a devoutly religious man, named them King David and Solomon. Blackwell once contemplated founding a Cherokee Strip town called City of David.

Through Blackwell's influence with the Cherokees, he was able to secure an ideal townsite for the proposed new town of Blackwell Rock. The Cherokee Strip Business and Protective Association managed to have the allotments of three Cherokee children set aside for a town. A court appointed a guardian for the children and ordered sale of their allotments to the company. Colonel Blackwell and the company were overjoyed, for the land was near the center of K county. They considered this an ideal location for the county seat.

With land for Blackwell Rock secured, the company sent Andrew J. Blackwell through southern Kansas promoting the town and selling certifi-

Blackwell citizens turned out en masse for the laying of the cornerstone of the Baptist State College on October 13, 1900. [Courtesy Cherokee Outlet Museum, Blackwell.]

cates for lots. A newspaper called the *Blackwell Eagle* was set up. It proclaimed the glories of the proposed new town. Thousands of copies were distributed to those awaiting the start of the run. Thus, on September 16, 1893, Blackwell Rock was ready to be settled.

The Race to Blackwell

Those who made the run to Blackwell Rock came mostly from the small town of Hunnewell, Kansas, whose population had grown from 200 to an estimated 20,000 on the day of the run. One settler recorded the temperature as 110 degrees as the massive, waving line formed for the race. No rain had fallen since April. Water was sold in buckets and barrels. Holes were dug in creek and river beds to find water. All along the line as far as the eye could see was a thick, rolling cloud of dust and ashes, for the prairie grass had been burned by soldiers to flush out Sooners.

At noon, rifle shots rang out along the line and the race was on. The distance to Blackwell Rock was about 20 miles. Some settlers never made it, and a number of dead horses were found in the Chikaskia River bed. A few settlers collapsed and fell asleep by an isolated water hole. But by early afternoon, Blackwell Rock was settled.

The citizens got busy immediately. Even while their faces were so covered with black ash they could scarcely recognize one another, they held a drawing for lots and elected temporary town officials.

Many Blackwellites obtained their college educations at the Baptist State College. It was the predecessor to Oklahoma Baptist University at Shawnee. The building was converted to a junior high school in the 1920s. [Courtesy Cherokee Outlet Museum, Blackwell.]

This frame building housed the Globe Mill, one of the earliest mills in Blackwell. It burned in the early 1900s. [Courtesy Cherokee Outlet Museum, Blackwell.]

The Electric Park Pavilion is one of Blackwell's historic buildings and pride of the city. Built in 1912 and 1913, the pavilion was for years the site of plays, community activities, and high school commencements. It now houses the Cherokee Outlet Museum operated by the Top of Oklahoma Historical Society. [Photo courtesy the Museum.]

Colonel Blackwell was chosen president of the town council and became the first mayor.

Stores, restaurants, and saloons sprang up in tents overnight. These were eventually replaced by wooden buildings when lumber was brought in from Hunnewell and Kildare. Within a month, Blackwell Rock boasted more than 100 business buildings.

All sorts of services were available, including those of seven well borers who dug wells and provided pumps and windmills. A community well was dug at the intersection of Main and Blackwell Streets. The town had three stage lines leading to nearby towns.

Two newspapers, the *Eagle* and the *Blackwell Rock Record* appeared on the first day. The latter, published by Homer S. Chambers, was the first to be produced in Blackwell Rock.

The Colonel Is Shrewd

Andrew J. Blackwell purchased an entire business block. On one corner he built the Blackwell Hotel, a tin three-story structure. He also built a non-denominational Union Church for use until each denomination could erect its own building. He preached the sermon at a dedication on July 1, 1894.

Firefighting with the bucket brigade ended in 1909 with the first fire department and modern fire wagon. The station entrance was on the south side of the city hall. The horses were Mac and Tim. [Courtesy Cherokee Outlet Museum, Blackwell.]

While he was known for his generosity in building a city, pioneers said Blackwell also had an eye for business. He managed to get his block divided into 13 lots instead of the usual 12. And before the run, he put up 300,000 tons of prairie hay. When the settlers arrived, the grass had been burned, and there was no feed for cattle. The settlers had to buy hay from Blackwell for $1.00 to $1.25 a bale, which they thought was exorbitant.

The *Times Record* noted that Col. Blackwell asked two dollars a month rent from a boy who was selling peanuts, popcorn, and cold drinks on his block. The boy refused to pay, but after some negotiation, he agreed to provide Blackwell with cold drinks on demand.

On November 21, 1893, the town had its first name change. The citizens voted 122 to 3 to incorporate and to change the name from Blackwell Rock to Blackwell. And on December 1 it was granted a post office under that name.

Blackwell Becomes Parker

Amid all the progress came a rude shock. In the late fall of 1893, E. S. Parker, who had made a small fortune marketing Parker's Titan Salve, established a new townsite just six miles south of Blackwell on the Chikaskia River. It was first called Chikaskia City and later Parker. The new community posed a threat to Blackwell and threatened to seek the county seat and a railroad stop.

The new townsite was so widely promoted that by the spring of 1894, the

Central School, Blackwell's first brick school, was built in about 1901 across from the city hall on West Blackwell Street. It started as a high school, but was later converted to a grade school. [Courtesy Cherokee Outlet Museum, Blackwell.]

This frame building was Lincoln School, built in 1911. It was near the high school on West Blackwell Street. [Courtesy Cherokee Outlet Museum, Blackwell.]

The Blackwell Steam Laundry at 306 North A Street had just acquired this horseless panel truck when this 1913 picture was taken. "We sew buttons" was its motto. [Courtesy Cherokee Outlet Museum, Blackwell.]

people of Blackwell were persuaded that it would be best to unite the two communities rather than to fight. To the surprise of many, on April 2, 1894, the name of the post office was changed from Blackwell to Parker.

The "marriage" of the two towns was not to last. The *South Haven, Kansas, New Era* reported in early May:

> The town of Blackwell, which was recently wed to the town of Parker and took upon itself the name of the worthy spouse "Parker," now regrets its hasty marriage and will sue for the restoration of its maiden name. Our sympathy is with Parker and we believe it ought to have alimony.

A bitter fight ensued between leaders of the towns. Colonel Blackwell sought the support of Blackwell people to buy up all lots in Parker. His dream was to have the town he founded named

Blackwell's Main Street had modernized considerably by 1914 but it was still teeming with buggies. This view is looking south from Oklahoma Avenue. [Courtesy Cherokee Outlet Museum, Blackwell.]

for him. Even the people of Parker were disillusioned at their own leaders and were ready to join Blackwell. The struggle ended on May 4, 1895 when the post office was renamed Blackwell.

The citizens of Blackwell were overjoyed and devoted themselves even more eagerly to building their schools, churches, businesses, and homes. Parker soon faded into obscurity, partly because it was almost washed away on several occasions by the high waters of the Chikaskia River and partly because it failed to interest railroads in a train stop there.

Shortly after Blackwell was settled, Colonel Blackwell said, "I will call this city Blackwell Rock and it will endure forever."He would be proud today of his "Rock" and the way it has endured for 100 years, still building and improving and serving as a beacon of optimism for the "Top of Oklahoma."

"Thirty Seconds Over Tokyo" was showing at the Rivoli theatre when this picture was taken in the early 1940s. Across the street was the J. C. Penney Co. and above Penneys was the Masonic Lodge. [Courtesy Cherokee Outlet Museum, Blackwell.]

TOP: Enid grew to impressive proportions, but the most devastating fire destroyed 30 buildings and the entire south side of the square on the night of July 13, 1901. Brick buildings quickly replaced the destroyed buildings. [Courtesy Darrel E. Keahey Collection.]

BOTTOM: Enid settlers thought the deliberate wrecking of this Rock Island train between 4 a.m. and 5 a.m. on July 13, 1894 was the making of Enid. [Courtesy Darrel E. Keahey Collection.]

Chapter Nine

Enid

"Queen City of the Outlet"

BEFORE THE DUST had settled on the Cherokee Strip run, some settlers at Enid were speaking of their new home as "Queen City of the Outlet." The name of their town fit well into that dream. Legends, probably true, say that Enid was named for the wife of Geraint, a bold knight of King Arthur's Roundtable. Geraint found Enid while trailing a scoundrel who had insulted Queen Guinevere.

Geraint stopped for lodging at the castle of the Earl of Yniol and while waiting in the castle court, he heard the earl's daughter, Enid, singing. He decided "Here, by God's grace, is the one voice for me." And the next day he said, "Having seen all beauties of our time, nor can see else where anything so fair...I will make her my true wife."

The knight carried out his mission and returned to Arthur's court, where he and Enid were wed. Enid and the queen became devoted to one another, the queen "arrayed and deck'd...Enid as the loveliest...in all the court" except for the queen.

As the story ends, Enid is called "Enid the fair" by the women and "Enid the good" by the people. Small wonder a Rock Island railroad official chose Enid for the name of a new city.

The Train Wouldn't Stop

During the Cherokee Strip run of 1893, most of the settlers of Enid came from Hennessey, about 20 miles south of there. Many of them were residents of Hennessey and of nearby Kingfisher. They had made the 1889 land run into Oklahoma, and now the grass in the Strip looked greener to them.

One participant estimated the number at Hennessey as 15,000. Many suffered and some died from lack of water in the searing heat. But as the guns fired starting the run, as many as 10,000 to 12,000 were packed into a seemingly endless string of cattle cars of a Rock Island train. The others ran beside the train in wagons, buggies, carts, and on horseback.

The settlers received a rude shock when the train reached their promised

In the Rock Island train incident, the engine and several cars passed over the sabotaged bridge, but five other cars tumbled from the track, spilling some fine Illinois seed wheat. Settlers grabbed all the wheat they could carry. [Courtesy Darrel E. Keahey Collection.

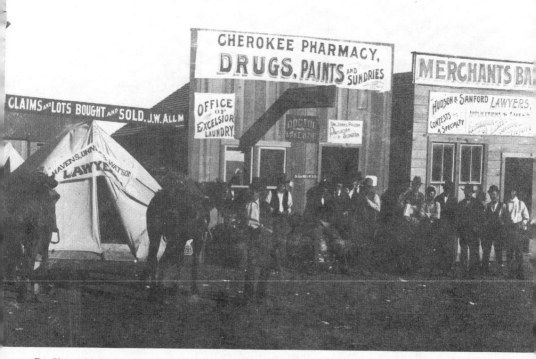

Dr. Henry McKenzie, Enid's first doctor, set up practice in the Cherokee Pharmacy building. As soon as he unpacked he began treating settlers who had jumped from the train. Lawyers set up business on both sides of the pharmacy. [Courtesy Darrell E. Keahey Collection.]

land—the Enid townsite. The train crew refused to stop at Enid. It proceeded three miles further north to the depot at North Enid. The latter had been originally planned for county seat of "O" County, but just before the opening, the government ordered the site switched to Enid. Thus, at the time of the opening, North Enid had a depot and a townsite laid out by the railroad. Enid had a post office, established on August 25, 1893, and a government square, but no depot.

Settlers tried in vain to stop the train at Enid, then some jumped while it was moving. Others went on to North Enid and wearily trudged back to Enid. There a 16 x 32 foot frame land office had been constructed on a corner of the government square and next to it was a post office set up in a tent. The first postmaster was Robert M. Patterson.

All Lots Claimed

From 10,000 to 15,000 people slept on the Enid townsite the first night. By nightfall, every platted lot in the 320-acre townsite had been taken. The original townsite extended from present Washington Street on the west to Tenth Street on the east and from Market Street on the south to Randolph on the north.

Those who envisioned Enid as "Queen City of the Outlet" had remarkable vision in 1893 for as far as the eye could see was a bald, unbroken, uninviting prairie. It resembled a desert more than the garden it became. But the set-

Garfield County's first courthouse is on the left and the first jail is at lower right in this early 1900s view of Haymarket Square. Notorious Cherokee Strip outlaw Nathaniel (Zip) Wyatt, alias Dick Yeager, died in this jail on September 6, 1895. [Courtesy Darrel E. Keahey Collection.]

TOP: Only a picture taken on Sunday morning could have found the north side of the square this quiet. [Courtesy Darrel E. Keahey Collection.]

BOTTOM: More than 30,000 tickets were sold for the Ringling Bros. circus performance in Enid in September 1897. To the right is the Hotel Rex, an early showplace. Few knew the veneer on the hotel was imitation sheet iron brick rather than the real thing. [Courtesy Darrel E. Keahey Collection.]

tlers set about immediately to make their dream come true.

At first nearly all homes and business structures were tents. Courthouse square was virtually covered with tents for county officers. Gradually frame buildings appeared, but many businesses operated in tents for months.

Territorial Governor William C. Renfrow called for a census of only those who intended to become permanent residents. The 5,200 who qualified could cast votes in the first election. John C. Moore was chosen the first mayor and he immediately organized a board of education. Subscription schools were set up, first in a tent on Independence Street and then in frame buildings scattered throughout the town. The first public school opened on March 12, 1894.

The Train Takes a Dive

One of Enid's greatest triumphs came with the establishing of a train depot on its first birthday, September 16, 1894. After the land run, the Rock Island had refused to stop in "South Enid," as Enid was known, even after angry settlers placed railroad ties, outhouses, and other debris on the tracks.

Finally a group of them cut the pilings under a train bridge between 4 a.m.

A large crowd gathered on the southeast corner of the square in the early 1900s to watch this parade of buggies. The view is looking south on Grand Avenue. [Courtesy Darrel E. Keahey Collection.]

and 5 a.m. on July 13, 1894. The next freight plunged into Boggy Creek. It took an act of Congress requiring trains to stop at all county seats and a proclamation by President Grover Cleveland to get the Rock Island to stop there.

The railroad fight caused great bitterness between the two Enid townsites and Mayor John C. Moore recorded in his memoirs:

> ...we all went armed to defend the city...from threatened danger of burning. Three hundred citizens were sworn in as special policemen, and patrolled the city night and day.

The two towns eventually buried the hatchet as they grew together. Pioneers say the winning of the railroad fight was the making of Enid.

As in most strip towns, newspapers quickly appeared in Enid. First was the *West Side Weekly Democrat* on September 19, 1893. This was followed two days later by the *Enid Daily Enterprise* and the *Enid Weekly Eagle. The Coming Events,* later the *Enid Events,* started in November, 1893, and then became the *Enid Daily Wave* in December.

Church leaders also moved quickly to get organized. The run was on Saturday, and on Sunday morning, most religious denominations held services on courthouse square. Soon they were meeting in tents and business buildings. Formal organization started with the First Christian Church in October. Methodists, Baptists, Presbyterians, and Episcopalians, and others organized early in 1894.

Thus Enid moved rapidly to become

Enid High School found its first real home in 1906 in this building at 106 East Independence. Earlier, it had been in a Baptist Church on East Cherokee, in Old Central Building, and in the old Opera House on East Broadway. [Courtesy Darrel E. Keahey Collection.]

"Queen City of the Outlet" as it became a center of agriculture, oil, education, and religious activity. And since 1893 it has been the largest city in the outlet.

TOP: One of Oklahoma's pioneer educational institutions was the Enid Business College, established in 1904 on the west side of the square. Many of its graduates became business leaders in the Cherokee Strip. [Courtesy Darrel E. Keahey Collection.]
BOTTOM: Hotel Donly, later to become the Hotel Rex, was built in 1894. The view is looking north on Independence Street. [Courtesy Darrel E. Keahey Collection.]

TOP: In this view of the west side of the square, the Hotel Rex has become the Hotel Feild. Note the water wagon in the center of the photograph washing down the street to settle dust. [Courtesy Darrel E. Keahey Collection.]

BOTTOM: The water wagon used to control dust on Enid streets was also an advertising medium. In background is the American Hotel, which in 1919 became the Oxford. It was destroyed by fire on June 15, 1978. [Courtesy Darrel E. Keahey Collection.]

TOP: One of Enid's earliest industries was the Vitrified Brick & Tile Company, established in the 1890s by the Frantz family near shale deposits on the south side. It became the Davies Brick Plant in 1943 and the Acme Brick Company in 1967. It closed in 1968. [Courtesy Darrel E. Keahey Collection.]

BOTTOM: The Watrous Drug Store at 125 South Grand was owned by Eugene Watrous. He later became a state senator and helped raise funds to start the Enid State School for the retarded. The First National Bank building replaced the drug store in 1907. As workers dug a basement for it, the saloon at left fell into the basement. [Courtesy Darrel E. Keahey Collection.]

TOP: This 1904 picture provides a long view of South Grand Avenue starting at the first block off the square with the early mills and Rock Island depot near the end. [Courtesy Darrel E. Keahey Collection.]

BOTTOM: Grand Avenue appears muddy in this 1904-05 scene, but board walks across it are an aid to foot traffic. [Courtesy Darrel E. Keahey Collection.]

This view from Main and Grand shows one of Enid's first laundry wagons and beyond it the two-story Rakestraw Building, the earliest auditorium used for community meetings. The entire block went up in flames in the 1901 fire. [Courtesy Darrel E. Keahey Collection.]

TOP: Shortly after Newkirk was settled, a crowd gathered around the Bank of Santa Fe. The town was first called Santa Fe, but the post office was changed to Newkirk on January 18, 1894. [Courtesy Newkirk Community Historical Museum.]

BOTTOM: From the earliest days wagon loads of wheat were a familiar sight on the Newkirk square. An estimated 450 loads were brought in on the day this photo was taken. [Courtesy Newkirk Community Historical Museum.]

Chapter Ten

Newkirk

Saloons Provided a Tax Base

To SUGGEST THAT any settlers in the Cherokee Strip run had an easy time would be a gross error, but those who headed for the town designated as the "K" county seat enjoyed a few favorable circumstances.

First, they were permitted to run from south edge of the Chilocco Indian Industrial School, which had been reserved by the government. This placed some of them only five miles from their destination. One settler made the run and staked his claim in only 14 minutes. Most of those running from the north or south borders of the Strip had to race pell-mell for more than an hour.

Those at Chilocco received another break. A nervous soldier fired the starting gun four minutes early, and the giant wave moved ahead of settlers in other locations. Still a third advantage came when they arrived and found a county government already operating.

Governor William C. Renfrow had appointed commissioners, a county clerk and a register of deeds. The town had been laid out neatly. Areas for residential lots, business lots, streets, parks, schools, and the courthouse were clearly marked and little confusion resulted. Bitter quarrels and fights ensued in conflicting claims for lots, and several shooting incidents were reported, but the violence was much less than that in other areas. Government cavalrymen were on hand to keep order.

How Newkirk Was Named

The government originally had decided to name the new county seat Lamoreaux to honor Secretary of the Interior S. L. Lamoreaux, who had directed the surveying of county seat towns in the Strip. However, the choice of a name brought about some confusion.

About three miles south of the line of the run was a hay station named Kirk with a train switch and a corral. Many of those making the run mistook this for the new county seat townsite. One settler estimated that as many as 5,000 dismounted and were staking out lots before they discovered their error. They finally arrived at the real townsite in the evening.

Two days after the run, a mass meeting was held to choose a name. Hopeful of getting a Santa Fe train depot, they enthusiastically decided to call the town Santa Fe. The railroad apparently was not flattered. Other towns named Santa Fe already existed. Shortly after that another meeting was held and Newkirk was selected as a name. The post office name was changed from Santa Fe to Newkirk on January 18, 1894, since the Kirk hay station had been abandoned. The Santa Fe post office had been established on October 5, 1893. For several weeks county newspapers referred to the town as Santa Fe. The first newspaper in Newkirk was called the *Lamoreaux*

Democrat, but after one issue it became the *Santa Fe Democrat*.

By evening of the first day, about 5,000 settlers were on the townsite. The next day Rev. B. C. Swartz of Arkansas City stood on a bale of hay on the courthouse lawn and conducted the first worship services. That same afternoon a Congregational minister from Arkansas City preached from a buggy on the square.

As Monday morning dawned, businesses were open in tents all around the square. Within a week, Newkirk boasted two hardware stores, two livery stables, two grocery stores, three saloons, three restaurants, a barber shop, a drug store, and two lumber yards. And already offering services were a doctor, three lawyers,

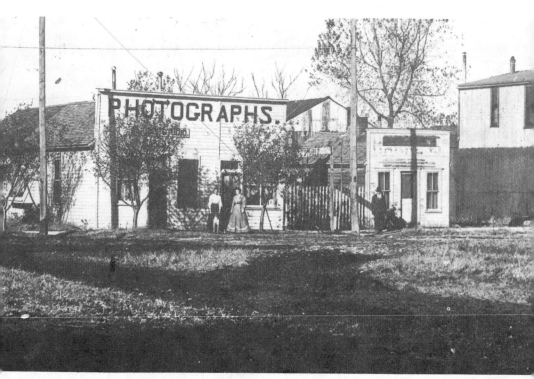

In most pioneer communities, men operated the photo studios. In Newkirk, Mrs. Ada Garside had one of the best equipped studios in the Strip. She took many of the early-day pictures of Newkirk and surrounding area. Her studio was on the west side of the square. [Courtesy Newkirk Community Historical Museum.]

several well-diggers, a stone mason, a blacksmith, an auctioneer, and several carpenters.

Saloons Provided Taxes

Newkirk's saloons may have been an asset, since the only revenue the new county government had was from saloon taxes and fines which often came from people patronizing the saloons. The county had no roads or machinery. Some settlers went to Kansas, borrowed road-grading machinery and then "forgot" to return it. In the beginning days, trips from farms into town and back were all day excursions.

In October 1893, Newkirk was designated a mail distribution center for the county, and mail was sent by stage to Blackwell and other locations. The town's population in town had dwindled to approximately 1,000 when it was incorporated on January 8, 1894.

Kay county's first courthouse was completed in 1894, but was destroyed by fire on March 4, 1897. A second frame courthouse was completed in the fall of 1897. The present courthouse was dedicated on October 28, 1926. It was built in the center of the square at a cost of $280,000.

A. M. Thomas, one of the first county commissioners, noted that the second bank was the Kay County bank that opened October 12, 1893, and that the first church built was the United Brethren. Thomas also noted that no provisions had been made for public schools,

After the 1893 run, businesses occupied all sides of the square at Newkirk. The Haynes building on the north end still stands, although modified, and houses the historical society's museum. [Courtesy Newkirk Community Historical Museum.]

TOP: Kay County's first courthouse was destroyed by fire on March 4, 1897. The second frame building, shown here, was completed in the fall of that year and lasted until the present courthouse was completed in 1926. [Courtesy Newkirk Community Historical Museum.]
BOTTOM: It's the morning after Newkirk's great fire in the fall of 1901 that destroyed the entire block of Main between Sixth and Seventh streets. The town had no fire-fighting equipment. In the center background is the courthouse. [Courtesy Newkirk Community Historical Museum.]

but a private school was operated by Thomas Pate with Mrs. Nellie Cook and Miss Ona Cochran as teachers.

Subscription schools in which parents "subscribed" and paid for their children's schooling were common in new Oklahoma towns even into the early 1900s. In Newkirk several such schools existed until the first free school system was established in January 1894. The first permanent school was a stone building erected in 1897, and the first high school was built in 1901.

On June 11, 1894, the city purchased lots for a cemetery, and on September 3 an ordinance was passed granting Northern Oklahoma Telephone Company permission to establish a phone system.

Winning the County Seat

It was 1899 before Newkirk's board of trustees called an election to authorize issuing $20,000 in water works bonds and decided to build a 100,000 gallon water tower. As in several other Strip villages, bucket brigades were used to fight fires, and merchants were required to keep two barrels of water in front of their stores. This changed in Newkirk in

This meat market on the square gave Newkirk settlers a chance not only to see what they were buying but to squeeze on the meat to see if it was fresh. [Courtesy Newkirk Community Historical Museum.]

1901 when fire destroyed the east side of Main Street between Sixth and Seventh Streets. The town got busy and purchased new fire-fighting equipment.

Newkirk's most important victory came in 1908 just after Oklahoma had been granted statehood. Blackwell and Ponca City both wanted to be the county seat, and an election was held to settle the matter. Newkirk and Blackwell edged out Ponca City in a fall election, but none of the three towns had a majority. When a run-off election was held in December 1908, Newkirk was chosen over Blackwell by a vote of 2,709 to 2,659. On January 30, 1912, the State Supreme Court proclaimed Newkirk the county seat.

With this victory and its rich agricultural area, Newkirk began its growth into a legal center and agricultural hub of one of Oklahoma's outstanding counties.

Like a Rock of Gibraltar, the Eastman National Bank has stood for 100 years. The first bank in Kay County and now the oldest, it started as the Bank of Santa Fe in October 1893, founded by E. B. Eastman. It changed to Eastman National Bank in 1908. The bank moved to this building at Seventh and Main shortly after 1900. It was still there at this writing. [Courtesy Newkirk Community Historical Museum.]

TOP: After the 1893 land run, the Santa Fe closed its station at Kirk and established a stop at Newkirk on its main line from Kansas City to Fort Worth. This station served until 1916 when a new brick structure replaced it. [Courtesy Newkirk Community Historical Museum.]

BOTTOM: Newkirk's first permanent school building opened in 1897. Its first schools were subscription schools, but a free system began in January 1894 and the first permanent school building (above) was opened in 1897. [Courtesy Newkirk Community Historical Museum.]

Waiting for the signal on the south
line of the Strip Sep 16th 93

TOP: The big land rush to Perry starts from Orlando. Even the top of the first train is crowded with settlers. Sooners hiding near Cow Creek beat them to Perry. [Courtesy H. E. Ricker family.] BOTTOM: A mixture of dust and ashes kept Perry settlers coated with grime after the run. The first tent on the right is the Blue Bell Saloon, which opened for business the first day. [Courtesy Kansas State Historical Society.]

Chapter Eleven

Perry

Thousands Jammed Hell's Half Acre

ALTHOUGH CHAOS and suffering prevailed at all points of the north and south borders of the Cherokee Strip on September 16, 1893, the greatest confusion probably existed in the settlement of Perry in county "P", which later became Noble County.

Although some settlers purchased train tickets at Arkansas City to come to Perry from the north, the largest number by far gathered at Orlando about eleven miles south. Orlando, like Stillwater, was a small village created after the run of 1889. Now, thousands of settlers swarmed into the two towns to make the run northward.

Estimates ranged from 15,000 to 25,000 on the number at Orlando. Among them were many of their own townspeople looking to greener pastures in the Strip. As many as 12,000 of these boarded trains for the run. Heat, dust, and ashes brought suffering to Orlando, and water sold for twenty-five cents a glass.

On the eve of the run leaflets, supposedly from the land office, circulated that Block "A" in Perry would be open

for settlement but that Block "B" to south was closed. This proved to be a hoax that caused heartaches and confusion.

Then on September 16, a soldier at Orlando accidentally fired his gun three minutes early and the great rush started ahead of time. As the masses converged on Perry, they encountered another surprise. The townsite was already swarming with claimants who apparently had been hiding near Cow Creek several miles south of town.

Visibility—Twenty Feet

No trees or foliage existed on the townsite and a cloud of black dust stirred by the run hung over the area. Frustrated settlers found visibility limited to 20 feet as they tried to locate claims.

Most of these faithfully obeyed instructions on the leaflet. They passed up Block "B" and crowded onto the Government Acre. In a matter of hours the square was jammed with hundreds of crude business structures. In the meantime, favored claimants took advantage of the hoax and occupied Block "B". The government ordered all occupants off Government Acre and they had to find new locations.

On the southwest corner of the acre square was a rickety frame building housing the post office, which had been established on August 25, 1893. Perry was named for J. A. Perry, one of the townsite location commissioners. "P" County became Noble County, named for John W. Noble, Secretary of the Interior.

By nightfall, an estimated 20,000 homesteaders had jammed into Perry. Most of them tried to register their claims at the land office, just east of Government Acre in a notorious section known as Hell's Half Acre. The entire block was covered by saloons, dance halls, restaurants, and law offices. A Wichita *Eagle* reporter described the scene:

There are sixty-nine saloons at Perry ... They are combination gin mills, dance houses and gambling dens ...The sheriff ordered one saloon not to sell a few nights ago and the proprietor got mad, saddled a horse, rode around town and announced he had 500 bottles of beer to give away ...An immense crowd gathered at his place and before 12 o'clock 500 empty bottles were lying around.

The *Eagle* reported that on Sunday morning, a church, a gambling house and a dance hall were all operating on the same lot and all were doing "a rushing business."

More than 100 lawyers had flocked to Perry for divorce and land claims business. Only a 90-day residency was required for divorces and many individuals stayed in Perry boarding houses for that period. As many as 3,000 land con-

Crowds gathered around the Perry post office after the run. [Courtesy Oklahoma Historical Society, neg. #8408.]

tests brought lawyers other clients. Almost every lot had from two to a dozen claimants.

Lines at the land office were so long that numbers were handed out. Positions in line were immediately sold for prices up to $500. Soon, settlers were able to buy their way into the office and get claims settled without a delay. This practice ended when a land office employee was charged with bribery.

In spite of confusion and hardships, Perry's hardy pioneers wasted no time building their town. On the night of the land run, camp fires and torch lights flickered throughout the vast encampment. By morning Perry had a business district, and many individuals had fash-ioned make-shift homes. One report stated that, within a short time, Perry had 28 lumber yards and 62 grocery stores.

Beer—A Dollar a Bottle

Water was at a premium, but the Buckhorn saloon brought in 38,000 bottles of beer which sold for one dollar each the first day and fifty cents the second. The government had dug one well at Brogan and Flynn streets and a spring on A street provided some drinking water. Settlers quickly dug wells at their homes.

A $60,000 water bond issue for a waterworks system and cemetery passed

Pioneers were never too busy to pray. Worship services were held outdoors the morning after the run. Some men were on horseback at this service on October 8, 1893. [Courtesy Oklahoma Historical Society, neg. #15021.]

on February 26, 1894. A waterworks and electric system was completed on July 20, 1895. Immediately after the waterworks came a fire department with a horse-drawn truck. Until then, a bucket brigade coped with fires. Each business was required to have two barrels of salt water and several buckets in front.

John Brogan, a Democrat, was elected Perry's first mayor on October 21, 1893. One of his first acts was to bring in two lawmen who later won fame as peace officers. Deputy marshal William M. Tighlman came from Guthrie and was named chief of police. Heck Thomas became one of Perry's first policemen.

ABOVE: Hell's Half Acre appears quiet in this picture, although a crowd has gathered around the Buckhorn Saloon (the center tent where flag is flying), where 38,000 bottles of beer were brought in and sold for a dollar each. [Courtesy Oklahoma Historical Society, neg. #19255a.]

RIGHT: Perry's homesteaders were considerate of the women. This "Ladies Water Closet" was set up on the edge of the courthouse square. [Courtesy Kansas State Historical Society.]

E. W. Jones, Perry's earliest historian, ridiculed the tales of violence and heroic actions of peace officers as creations of writers. He wrote:

> Of the sundry and numerous outlaws laid low by the trusty guns of Tighlman, and Thomas..there is no record and research fails..to locate a grave, marked or unmarked, where rests a single body of the died-with-their-boots-on contingent...

A frame 70-by-100-foot courthouse was built in 1894 with a stone jail in the rear. The acre then became known as courthouse square.

The Depot Comes to Town

Perry achieved a special triumph in the spring of 1894. Until then, the Santa Fe train passed through town and stopped only at the Wharton depot one mile south. After Perry passed an ordinance limiting train speed to four miles an hour through town, the depot was moved to Perry.

In the summer of 1894, bonds in the sum of $20,260 were issued for construction of a high school and two ward schools. Relatively few children were in Perry until then, and they had been attending subscription schools in scattered business buildings.

Carl Malzahn came to Perry in 1902 and in 1903 established his blacksmith shop in this building. It was the beginning of the great enterprise now known as Charles Machine Works, Inc. Gustave, (1) and Charlie, his sons, took over the shop after Carl died in 1913. The building has been modified but still stands in the 200 block of East Sixth Street. [Courtesy Charles Machine Works, Inc.]

Newspapers sprang up in Perry on the first day. Lon Wharton brought his *Perry Sentinel* to town from Chandler on the first day. Bert Green started the *Perry Times*, a daily and weekly, also on September 16. The *Perry Democrat* followed a few days later. A number of others started and soon folded.

Perry endured its suffocating dust until the spring of 1895 when the ground was planted with alfalfa. And a year later, Will T. Little planted 8,600 elm tree sprouts in strategic places.

With this groundwork laid, the pioneers of Perry set about to build a town that has been known for a century for its friendliness, hospitality, outstanding schools, athletes, and churches.

This intersection on North Sixth Street was called Brewery Corner two weeks after the land run. Next to the Pabst Brewing Co. was a short-order cafe. Construction was underway all along the block. [Courtesy Oklahoma Historical Society, neg. #8400.]

TOP: This 1893 view of Perry was taken from C Street and Sixth looking northwest. The dusty streets had turned to mud on this day. [Courtesy Oklahoma Historical Society, neg. #8422.]
BOTTOM: Frame buildings had replaced tents when this view of northwest Perry and Government Acre was taken in October 1893. Outhouses are in small tents near many of the buildings. [Courtesy Oklahoma Historical Society, neg. #8417.]

ABOVE: The spring at South Avenue and
Thirteenth Street where Burton S. Barnes
camped in 1893 still flows and is one of
Ponca City's historic sites. [Photo by author.]
RIGHT: On Monday, April 24, 1895, Ponca
City citizens turned out en masse for a giant
parade and evening ball to honor their
"gifted mayor and founder," Burton
Seymour Barnes. [From *The Last Run*,
courtesy Ponca City Chapter, D.A.R.]

Chapter Twelve

Ponca City

One Man's Dream Came True

WHEN SHOTS rang out to start the Cherokee Strip run, eleven trains carrying 12,000 frantic settlers moved into the county designated as "K". On each side of them were thousands of individuals in prairie schooners, buggies, or on horseback. Some of the hopefuls headed toward Newkirk. Others, especially some on trains, sought land near Perry. But the largest number planned to stake claims in the vicinity of Cross, where a townsite had been laid out, a post office was established, and a train station was operating.

In spite of the government's carefully made plans, one man had his own ideas about where a town ought to be. Burton Seymour Barnes had been a furniture manufacturer in Adrian, Michigan, but in 1892, the depression caused him to sell his business.

Excited as he read of the forthcoming Strip opening, Barnes decided to explore the land. He was already dreaming of founding a new town. He took the train to Arkansas City where he purchased a surrey and two sturdy black horses. From there he drove through the eastern edge of the Strip, studying land around the proposed townsites of Enid, Perry, and Cross.

He Finds the Spring

From Perry, Barnes drove north through the Otoe and Ponca Indian reservations. After leaving the latter, he came to a spring at the site of present day 13th Street and South Avenue. He rested for awhile, and as he sipped the fresh water, he saw a freight train passing about a mile away. According to his memoirs, Barnes exclaimed, "This is the site for a new city. With such good water and a location on the railroad near the river crossing, it is an ideal site for a city." He organized the Ponca Townsite Company and sold 2,300 certificates at two dollars each. These would entitle the holder to first call on lots as original owners offered them for sale. The money was to be used for surveying, laying out the new townsite, and organizing a city government.

On the day of the run, Barnes with

his surrey and black horses was among the thousands in line. As a soldier fired his carbine skyward, the line moved forward like a giant wave. The trains, with whistles blowing and bells clanging, moved with it. Traveling about 12 miles an hour, the trains slowed down near section lines and settlers jumped off to run for claims. Some turned somersaults as they hit the ground.

Barnes had the advantage over most of the settlers. He knew where he was going and how to get there. He went directly to the southeast corner of the section he had chosen for Ponca City. Eight others staked claim to the land, but Barnes won the contest over some of them and settled with others for a small payment.

Lots and Blocks Laid Out

The dust had hardly settled after the run when efforts began to establish a new town. No townsite had been set aside in advance as with Cross, Perry, and Enid. Following through on the Ponca Townsite Co. plan, 2,000 homesteaders gathered two days after the run and secured a section of land by purchasing releases from all who had made claims to them. Surveyors went to work and in two days the section was staked off in lots and blocks. The result was 194 blocks with 20 lots in each block.

On Thursday morning, September 21, a drawing was held to determine which block each townsite member would have. The members had agreed to

After the drawing for lots on September 21, 1893, buildings mushroomed on Grand Avenue, including a water tank near First Street. [Courtesy Pioneer Woman Museum, Ponca City.]

abide by the drawing. That night, the settlers held their first election, choosing Barnes as mayor, J. W. Dalton as treasurer, and W. G. Cronkwright as clerk.

Within a few days frame business buildings appeared on Grand Avenue, which had been designated the principal street. The new town seemed on its way to success, but one major obstacle had to be resolved.

Ponca City was only one mile south of Cross and a bitter fight emerged to determine which would survive. With its depot, post office, and express office, Cross seemed to have the advantage.

Jibes were exchanged and altercations occurred as Poncans went to Cross to pick up mail or to catch trains.

The Exodus from Cross

Again, the Ponca citizens found an answer. They persuaded the train agent at Cross to seek a transfer to Ponca City. At night they moved his house to lots on Fourth Street. Barnes then purchased the Midland Hotel at Cross and moved it to Ponca City. Later the Arcade Hotel was moved from Cross to First Street and

Ponca City's Grand Avenue had become impressive when this snow scene was taken about 1901. The view is looking west from Fourth Street. On the left is the city's first daily newspaper, the Ponca City Courier. Across the street are the Planter Hotel and the grocery store operated by Louis S. Barnes, son of Burton S. Barnes. [Courtesy Velma and Ray Falconer.]

TOP: It took a bitter fight, but Ponca City finally won a Santa Fe train stop. The town celebrated wildly as the first train rolled in at 9:27 a.m. on Saturday, September 22, 1894. [From *The Last Run*, courtesy Ponca City Chapter, D.A.R.]

BOTTOM: The Arcade Hotel was important in Ponca City's history. The original frame hotel was hauled from the Cross townsite to First and Grand and helped establish Ponca City as the dominant town. The modernized Arcade above became the home of oilman and philanthropist Lew Wentz. The Arcade was torn down in 1974. [Courtesy Pioneer Woman Museum.]

Grand Avenue. This started a general exodus, and Cross citizens watched angrily as most of their business district eventually moved south.

Ponca City's first post office was established January 12, 1894 as New Ponca. The name was changed to Ponca on July 7, 1898, and finally to Ponca City on October 23, 1913. The great triumph came in September 1894 when the Santa Fe railroad authorized a stop in Ponca City.

Water was a severe problem in the beginning. A kindly handicapped man, Billy Evans, provided temporary relief by hauling water in barrels and selling it for 15. cents a barrel. Soon the city dug a well in the center of Grand Avenue near Fourth Street with a windmill and large tank. The city did not have an official water system until 1898.

In late 1894, the Northern Oklahoma Telephone Company brought Ponca City its first phone service from a building at Second and Grand Avenue. Thirty families subscribed. Within six weeks after the run, a school house had been completed.

With all of these achievements, the pioneers of Ponca City set about building their town. Like most towns of that era, Ponca City was described as a "wild, rip-roaring town," but as years went by it grew into a cultured, sophisticated, gracious small city, certainly one of Oklahoma's finest.

Fixtures, ornaments and pictures appear almost elegant in this early-day Ponca City barber shop. The young barber in the last chair is the only gentleman without a handlebar moustache. [Courtesy Western History Collections, University of Oklahoma Library.]

Ponca City became a city of grace, culture, and sophistication, and much of this is attributed to Ernest W. Marland (right), oil man, philanthropist, and patron of the arts. Marland came to Oklahoma in late 1908 and in a few years his oil exploration had brought him an estimated $30 million. He gave generously to many facets of Ponca City life. He was elected to Congress in 1932, and was governor of Oklahoma from 1934 to 1938. Marland lost his wealth during the Great Depression of 1929, but his contributions to Ponca City left the city rich in culture for generations to come. [Photo courtesy Velma and Ray Falconer.]

A native of Pittsburg, Pa., Lew Haines Wentz came to the Ponca City area in January 1911. He eventually became wealthy from oil leases in the Three Sands field. Wentz became known for his philanthropies and helping needy young people. He bought toys and clothing for hundreds of children, financed the Crippled Childrens Hospital in Oklahoma City, and built Ponca City's $200,000 Boy Scout camp. He made loan funds available for needy students at both Oklahoma and Oklahoma State Universities. The above scene was at the hospital. [Courtesy Pioneer Woman Museum, Ponca City.]

TOP: This beautiful Civic Center graces the 500 block of East Grand Avenue in Ponca City. The auditorium was built in 1917 and the two wings added in 1923. A statue of E. W. Marland is in the foreground. [Photo by author.]

BOTTOM: When the Jens-Marie Hotel was built in 1924 in the 100 block of North Second Street, it was considered one of the finest in the Cherokee Strip and headquarters for many celebrities. The hotel was demolished at 8:40 a.m. on January 9, 1978, on a bitterly cold day. It collapsed in five seconds. [Courtesy Velma and Ray Falconer.]

TOP: The most familiar historic site in Ponca City is the Pioneer Woman Statue. The statue was unveiled on April 22, 1930 before 40,000 people. More than 20,000 visitors come annually to the Pioneer Woman Museum in the background at right. [Photo by author.]

BOTTOM: One of Ponca City's historic treasures is the Poncan Theatre, built in 1927 at a cost of $280,000. Efforts have been underway for several years to restore the building. [Photo by author.]

Chapter Thirteen

Woodward

The Pioneers Survive Blizzards and Bobcats

As C. M. HALL DISMOUNTED from his Texas cow pony in Woodward in early afternoon of September 16, 1893, he gazed in awe at the sight before him. Over the hill to the south came an estimated 700 horses, their hoofbeats creat-

The frame building that housed the Woodward land office was well equipped on the inside. It had modern desks, a typewriter, a pot-bellied stove, and a calendar with George Washington's picture. It was built by W. H. Wiggins. [Courtesy Western History Collections, University of Oklahoma Library.]

ing a thunderous roar, their riders hell-bent on claiming lots in N County.

The first man to arrive in Woodward was David Jones, a resident of the Texas Panhandle. Behind him two other horsemen were in a dead heat for a quarter section adjoining the townsite on the east. After three minutes, nine other riders arrived and within another three minutes came the great avalanche of horsemen. And Hall reported "...when they did come the stampede of the bison or a cyclone from the southwest was imaginary in comparison."

The cow ponies had proved the margin of victory for many as they out-distanced imported thoroughbreds and brought their riders in ahead of the trains. Approximately 1,000 were on the townsite by the time the first train arrived with its 300 settlers.

The train failed to slow down until it reached the center of the townsite, but its riders began leaping from the top and sides several blocks earlier, many receiving broken bones and bruises. Immediately the struggle for town lots began. Fights occurred over some lots, but some settlers slipped out of the melee, walked a few feet, and claimed lots without incidents.

A Seven-Mile Line

The settling of N County was different in several ways from other land runs. Fortunately for the participants, the

Caravans of wagons brought broom corn into Woodward in the early days. Some farmers sold enough at harvest time to more than pay for their land. This 1905 photo shows Woodward had downtown electric lights. [Courtesy Western History Collections, University of Oklahoma Library.]

weather was more moderate, and on the day of the run a cool breeze swept through the encampments along the southern Strip border. Competition for land was generally not as severe as in the eastern part of the Strip. Some quarter sections were still unclaimed at the turn of the century.

Settlers also clustered for the run near border towns such as Arkansas City, Hunnewell, Caldwell, Orlando, and Stillwater. Those seeking homesteads in N

County were stretched out in a seven-mile line about 20 miles south of Woodward. Many others made the run by trains from Canadian and Higgins, Texas, or even from Kiowa, Kansas, on the northern border of the Strip. A few came from Dodge City and Ashland, Kansas, in covered wagons.

Joseph H. Cox made the run on a pack mule to Moscow Flats east of Woodward after he let his son, Eli, borrow his horse. Peter Martinson and his father,

The 1895 gunfight over a trivial court case was in the building just left of the Central Exchange Bank. Ed Jennings was killed and his brother, John, wounded from bullets fired by Temple Houston and Jack Love. [Courtesy Western History Collections, University of Oklahoma Library.]

Hans, rode double on a donkey to the Mutual area. Robert and Zelah Benn could probably claim the record for coming the furthest distance. They spent a year traveling from New Mexico, herding 3,000 Angora goats ahead of them.

Temple Houston Arrives

By train from Canyon, Texas, came Jerry R. Dean, where he had practiced law and served in the Texas legislature. He set up practice in a tent. On the train from Canadian, Texas, was another attorney, Sidney B. Laune, who had been practicing in Denver. Dean and Laune became partners, practiced law in Woodward for years, and became lifelong friends.

Also on the Canadian train was another man who was perhaps to become Woodward's most famous citizen. Temple Lea Houston, youngest son of Sam Houston, was 33 as he rode into Woodward on the rear platform of the train. He lived for only 12 years after his arrival, but each year of his Woodward life was turbulent and colorful. His gunfight with Ed and John Jennings in the Cabinet Saloon on August 8, 1895 is Woodward's most remembered legend.

The second story of the building built by Peter Martinson and H. A. Brockhaus served as a courtroom, opera house, and town meeting room. It was here that Temple Houston and Jack Love were acquitted in the slaying of Ed Jennings. [Courtesy Western History Collections, University of Oklahoma Library.]

Many of the settlers made no effort to claim Woodward town lots. They preferred farmlands where they could produce wheat, oats, barley, and broom corn. They formed communities such as Mutual, Dail City, that later became Mooreland, Curtis, Richmond, and Hackberry, which was later known as Sharon. Richmond's post office was established on November 6, 1893, and Curtis' was opened on October 3, 1894, but some of the small communities did not receive postal service until after 1900.

Fighting to Survive

The first settlers endured hardships almost beyond description. Building materials were not available on the vast unoccupied plains and families had to choose between dugouts and sod houses for homes. A few even continued to live in covered wagons.

The majority of them began life in dugouts of one or two small rooms. To protect their families from the cold, women placed quilts over the entrances and straw over the floors. Sheets across the ceilings kept dust from falling.

Prairie fires swept over the dugouts in the fall and heavy snowdrifts buried them in the winter. Settlers remained alert for coyotes and bobcats that roamed the prairie. Men often walked 15 miles or more into Woodward for supplies. Some homesteaders engaged in fights with ranchers who had been using the Strip for free grazing land. The cattlemen tore down settlers' fences and tried to discourage them from staying.

Some who made the run became discouraged and gave up their homesteads, but others found ways to survive.

A patron has one foot on the rail and his elbow on the bar, but no drink in hand, indicating this picture of the first saloon in Woodward was posed. The bartender is Buck Walsh. [Courtesy Western History Collections, University of Oklahoma Library.]

TOP: Angle parking seemed to prevail downtown at the turn of the century. The Central Hotel was on the corner of Ninth and Main Streets. [Courtesy Western History Collections, University of Oklahoma Library.]

BOTTOM. A 1991 photo shows things have changed considerably at the Ninth and Main intersection, but the corner buildings in this and the preceding picture have many of the same characteristics. [Photo by author.]

They worked in wheat harvests elsewhere or cut and sold fence posts from the canyons. Ed Childers sold windmills for $15 and installed them for another $18. George Bunch peddled water from his two springs in Woodward. Saraha Graves raised canaries and marketed them in the area. But those who stayed survived largely by helping one another. They shared food, clothing, and farm equipment. A county doctor made the rounds in a buggy to care for the sick.

Two Woodwards Arise

The townspeople of Woodward had their problems, too. As in Enid and Ponca City, the location of the townsite caused dissension. Even before the Strip run, a small settlement with a Santa Fe railroad station and post office existed there. The post office had been established on February 3, 1893 and was named for Brinton W. Woodward, a Santa Fe railroad director. The land office for registering claims had been built near the station in the summer of 1893.

When Col. Alfred P. Swineford of the General Land Office laid out the 320-acre Woodward townsite for the Strip run, he included this settlement. Later, he changed the location to a short distance west of there. The settlers were extremely confused and for a time two towns called East Woodward and West Woodward existed. To resolve all conflicts on the issue, a public meeting was held on December 28, 1893, and citizens of the two towns "united in an effort for peace and

Republicans were accused of employing all sorts of "dirty tricks" to try to keep Woodward voters from hearing popular William Jennings Bryan speak during the 1907 political campaign. But, he appeared in September before a large audience. [Courtesy Plains Indians and Pioneers Museum, Woodward.]

prosperity." The unification received greater impetus in August 1894 when Congress ordered the train depot moved to the official townsite. It eventually wound up between Fifth and Sixth streets just two blocks from the boundary of West Woodward.

The fuss over the location has special historical significance. As the town shifted west, it moved away from the public square which would have become the central business district. Woodward is today the only original county seat in the Cherokee Strip whose businesses are not centered around a courthouse square as decreed by Secretary of the Interior Hoke Smith. And the jog of Main Street at Eighth is caused by a lack of alignment of streets of the two Woodwards as they decided to join.

Woodward's first election was held Wednesday, September 20, 1893, and William B. Hale was chosen mayor. Only one slate of candidates was on the ballot. Voters had no choice, but 523 voted.

On November 18, 1894, voters chose Woodward as the name for N County. C. M. Hall, who boasted that his *Advocate* was the first newspaper in town, claimed credit for the choice and rejoiced that another proposed name, Eureka, had been eliminated.

A year after the run, Woodward had moved ahead rapidly. Frame buildings had replaced tents and dugouts. Transients had departed, and its 700 dedicated citizens were busy building their town. Among its business enterprises were two banks, four large general

Woodward people turned out en masse on March 9, 1912, to welcome the first passenger train over the Wichita Falls Railroad. [Courtesy Western History Collections, University of Oklahoma Library.]

stores, five hotels, five restaurants, four livery stables, and three lumber yards.

In addition to these were two physicians, three printing offices, a blacksmith shop, two churches, and two barber shops. One business outnumbered the rest. Woodward had seven saloons, and the *Advocate* said there were "carpenters and lawyers too numerous to mention."

With all this progress in the short time since the run, Woodward was ready to seek its destiny as Oklahoma's gateway to the West.

TOP: When statehood came in 1907, Woodward staged a parade, even though the county was being partitioned to create Harper and Ellis counties. [Courtesy Western History Collections, University of Oklahoma Library.]
BOTTOM: Loud, wide ties, double-breasted suits, and short lapels were in vogue as Harrison & Littrell Men's Clothing Store in Woodward displayed its fall merchandise in September 1916. [Courtesy Western History Collections, University of Oklahoma Library.]

TOP: The Miller Brothers, George S., Zack T., and Joe C., operated the great 101 Ranch after the death of their father, George W. Miller on April 25, 1903. All three were eventually designated honorary colonels by Oklahoma governors. [Courtesy Oklahoma Historical Society, neg. #20419.]

BOTTOM: This mansion known as "The White House" was the Miller Brothers home on the 101 Ranch. This is a 1928 photo. Courtesy Oklahoma Historical Society, neg. #21478.]

Chapter Fourteen

The 101 Ranch

"Magic Empire" of the Cherokee Strip

OTHER THAN the great land run itself, the most publicized and exciting aspect of the Cherokee Strip was the fabulous 101 Ranch. Sprawling over 110,000 acres on the Salt Fork River southwest of Ponca City, the ranch has been described as a "zoo, saddle shop, diversified farm, cattle ranch, Indian village, buffalo herd, apple orchard, poultry house, dairy, pickle works, oil refinery, and a lavish center for southern hospitality." It was all of these and more.

For more than 30 years it attracted celebrities from America and abroad. Col. William F. Cody (Buffalo Bill), performed for a year in the ranch's Wild West Show. Tom Mix was a cowboy there long before he became a movie hero. Geronimo, famed Apache chief, appeared in the 101's first Wild West Show; Jess Willard, heavyweight boxing champion, once traveled with the show.

Edna Ferber found material for her novel, "Cimarron," while visiting the ranch. John Philip Sousa and his band played there, and Will Rogers performed his rope tricks in his early career. Authors who visited the 101 included Rex Beach, Irvin S. Cobb, and Mary Roberts Rinehart.

Famous political figures who came to visit included Presidents Theodore Roosevelt and Warren G. Harding. Among others who came to the Strip to see the ranch were General John J. Pershing, William Jennings Bryan, Harry Sinclair, John Ringling, William Randolph Hearst, John D. Rockefeller, and William Allen White. As many as 100,000 visitors came to the 101 each year.

The ranch's story began to unfold in 1870, 13 years before the Strip opening. George Washington Miller, then 29, decided to give up management of his grandfather's farm in Crab Orchard, Kentucky, and to seek his dream of a large livestock ranch in the West. His goal was California.

Miller and his wife, Mary (Mollie), packed all their belongings into a covered wagon and with their two-year-old son, Joe, began their trek. As they passed through Mississippi and Missouri and reached the Kansas plains, Miller suddenly realized that here might be his dream—a cattle country virtually without cattle.

He and Mollie stopped for the winter at Newtonia, Missouri. Through trading and use of some of his capital, Miller went to Texas, acquired about 400 head of cattle, and drove them back to Baxter Springs. He found the country so suitable for grazing that he decided to stay.

He established his first ranch south of Baxter Springs on the Quapaw reservation near present day Miami, Oklahoma. The ranch was first known as the L-K Ranch, named for his partner, Lee Kokernut. While Miller operated the ranch, his family remained at Newtonia. A daughter, Alma, was born to the Millers on June 21, 1875, their second son, Zachary Taylor, was born on April 26, 1878. In 1880, Miller moved the family to Baxter Springs where a third son, George Lee, was born on September 9, 1881.

The Ranch Becomes 101

In 1879, Miller took an important step. He leased 60,000 acres in the Cherokee Strip for grazing purposes, and the following year he bought Kokernut's interest in the ranch and renamed it the 101. The origin of the name is uncertain. One tale says the 101 was the name of a San Antonio bar patronized by cowboys. Another is that it was taken from the Bar-O-Bar ranch in Oklahoma. The latter's brand was - O - Bar and Miller turned the bars vertically to make them more visible and they appeared as 101.

The Ponca Indians were always welcome guests at the 101 Ranch. These chiefs were en route to a celebration there. [Courtesy Oklahoma Historical Society, neg. #8665.]

In the same year, Miller built an elaborate home for his family at Winfield in southern Kansas.

Soon, historic events began to affect the 101 Ranch future. In 1878, the Ponca Indians were moved from Nebraska and settled temporarily on the Quapaw reservation near the 101 Ranch. Many of the Indians became ill and homesick. They were unhappy and wanted to return to Nebraska. Their chief, White Eagle planned a trip to Washington to protest the transfer.

Miller had become friends with the Poncas and he persuaded White Eagle to

Most famous of the Ponca chiefs was White Eagle. His friendship with George W. Miller made possible a lease for the 101 Ranch to locate in the Cherokee Strip. [Courtesy Velma and Ray Falconer Collection.]

look at the land which the government had tentatively set aside for the Poncas in the Strip. The chief and a delegation of tribesmen rode into the Strip, were impressed with the vegetation, streams and rivers, and decided to stay. Their reservation in the Strip was more than 101,000 acres.

This soon was to prove a great blessing for Miller, for after the Oklahoma land run of 1889, pressures grew to open the Cherokee Strip to homesteading. Foreseeing this, Miller leased thousands of acres of Ponca Indian reservation land from his friend, White Eagle.

When President Benjamin Harrison ordered all cattle removed from the Strip, Miller was ready. During the fall and winter of 1892, he moved his cattle and headquarters down the Salt Fork River to the Ponca reservation. When the lease with the Poncas was approved in Washington, the ranch headquarters were erected in a bluff on the south bank of the Salt Fork. The great 101 Ranch was now established.

Another historical event of 1893 at first seemed tragic but Miller turned it into a blessing. The great business panic of that year left the 101 penniless and deeply in debt after a Kansas City commission house failed and deprived Miller of $300,000 due him for cattle already sold.

"The Eastern bankers sent in men who took all of our cattle, "Zack Miller said later. "...When they got through, all we had left was 88 old horses and a handful of cows. We were as flat as the prairie."

They Turn to Farming

As Miller sat with his wife, Mollie, and his three young sons and planned for the future, an idea emerged. Why not diversify and turn to farming? Their herds had numbered in the thousands. Why not produce bushels by the thousands? In the spring of 1894, the Millers planted nearly 5,000 acres in wheat. This yielded 70,000 bushels that sold for $1.20 a bushel.

In 1903, the Millers were able to buy thousands of acres they had been leasing from the Poncas. The government had for several years been breaking up Indian reservations and making individual allotments to tribal members. Tribes could sell land only with government approval. White Eagle was able to secure approval of the sale to Miller.

This enabled the family to build permanent quarters on the spread, which with its owned and rented land, grew to 110,000 acres. The family home was called the White House. The ranch included parts of Kay, Noble, Osage, and Kay counties, and on its grounds were the small communities of Bliss, Red Rock and White Eagle, the latter on the edge of present Ponca City.

On April 25, 1903, Col. George W.

Miller died of pneumonia at age 61 and his sons took over management of the operation. Joe was now 35, Zachary (Zack) 25, and George Lee, 21. The sons had participated in the planning and decisions and they were ready for their new responsibilities.

Each son handled the tasks he loved best. Joe delighted in caring for the fields and orchards; Zack enjoyed buying, selling, and raising horses and cattle. Young George was talented as a business executive. He organized the offices and departments and maintained contacts with the outside world. In time, all three were designated colonels by Oklahoma governors. The 101 became widely known as the Miller Brothers 101 Ranch.

The First Big Show

The first challenge for the Miller Brothers came June 5-11, 1905 when they presented a wild west show for the National Editorial Association. Even the Millers were amazed as spectators

MILLER BROS. 101 RANCH, THE HOME OF

Headquarters Miller Bros., 101 Ranch, Bliss, Oklahoma, th

A panoramic view of the 101 Ranch shows the White House on the right and the general store on the left. [Courtesy Oklahoma Historical Society, neg. #6519.]

flocked in on 30 special trains, horses and wagons. Attendance estimates ranged from 50,000 to 100,000, the former probably being more accurate. Among the attractions was Geronimo, the Apache chief.

With such success and national publicity, the Millers organized a traveling show that performed in many cities over the nation from 1906 to 1914. The show was then taken to London, Berlin, and Paris, but as World War I began, the show was forced to end its overseas performances, although it made several appearances in American cities until 1916.

Over the years, the brothers continued to diversify. They added a tannery, a packing house, a laundry, a dairy, and even a circus. And in 1924 a terrapin derby became a part of the 101 annual attractions. The terrapins raced from the center of a 100-foot circle.

In 1922, wealth from oil was added to other income. Oil exploration had been going on since 1908, largely by Ernest W. Marland, who was persuaded to come from Pittsburg, Pa., to explore.

As several gas producing wells were brought in, other oil speculators were attracted to the area.

Watchorn Strikes Oil

Several oil producing wells had been discovered as early as 1911, but the big break-through on the 101 Ranch came in the spring of 1922 when Watchorn Oil Company headed by Robert Watchorn struck oil at 2,740 feet and the well became a major producer as drilling reached the Wilcox sand. The well was called the George L. Miller No. 1. In 1923, oil income on the ranch was $1,300,000, and oil wells dotted the landscape. The Millers set up their own refinery and became known as major operators.

Meanwhile, the agricultural production of the 101 was staggering. Five thousand acres were planted in corn, 4,000 in wheat, and 2,500 in cotton. The gross income of the ranch in 1925 was $1,070,512.

Thousands of cattle, horses, mules

IE 101 RANCH REAL WILD WEST SHOW.

est Diversified Farm and Ranch in the United States.

and hogs lived on the ranch's pasture lands. The magnitude of the operation may be illustrated by a trip Zack and George Miller made to Florida in 1927 where they purchased 9,000 head of cattle and shipped them to the 101.

One may wonder how such a magnificent empire, built brilliantly over more than a quarter century, could disintegrate rapidly, but a series of tragedies beginning in 1927 sent the 101 into a rapid decline. On October 21, 1926, Col. Joe C. Miller, the oldest brother, died at age 59. His death was caused by carbon monoxide gas while he was working on his automobile. Zack and George attempted to continue the traveling Wild West Show, but without Joe's management, it lost money and became heavily in debt.

A year of drought followed his death and the agricultural income dropped. Then on February 1, 1929, Col. George Lee Miller was killed as his car slid off a slippery road between Ponca City and the ranch. He was pinned beneath the car for two hours and died before reaching a hospital.

The Empire Collapses

While Zack, the surviving brother, was trying to bring ranch business and finances under control, the great stock market crash came in October 1929 followed by the depression of the 1930s. Prices of farm products, oil, and livestock plummeted to new lows. As income dropped, the cost of operation and taxes continued. The ranch recorded a net loss of $301,000 in 1929.

Most of the ranch's assets had been heavily mortgaged and creditors began to demand payment. Zack sought to negotiate with creditors, but on August 27, 1931, a suit was filed to place the ranch in receivership. The appointment of Fred C. Clarke as receiver was approved on September 16, and the control of the ranch was taken from the Miller family.

On March 24, 1932, Clarke at-

Thousands of head of cattle grazed on the 101 Ranch pasture lands. Colonel Zack Miller is tending this herd. [Courtesy Oklahoma Historical Society, neg. #14296.]

tempted to dispose of the ranch's assets at a public sale. While several thousand potential buyers milled around the ranch, Zack barricaded himself inside the ranch White House. Armed with a shotgun, he defiantly tried to stall the auction of the ranch property. He was subdued and jailed at the Kay County courthouse in Newkirk. He was saved from prosecution by Gov. William H. Murray, who sent a contingent of national guardsmen to Newkirk to free Miller. Murray said no one would be imprisoned during his administration for non-payment of a debt.

Miller made another last-ditch effort to save the ranch. His creditors approved a reorganization plan that gave him two years to restore the ranch and to raise money to pay off $700,000 in loans. This, too failed. On March 29, 1937, Miller gathered his few remaining possessions and sadly abandoned his beloved ranch.

Col. Zack Miller died on January 3, 1952 in Waco, Texas at age 74. His body was returned and buried on the grounds of the 101. Thus ended the 101 Ranch, the proud empire of the Cherokee Strip. Few remnants of the ranch are visible from Highway 156 that winds past there. The ranch store burned in 1987 and the blacksmith shop burned on September 24, 1991, leaving only two dilapidated barns to mark the ranch site.

ABOVE: Cowboys, cowgirls and ranch hands are gathered around the 101 Ranch cafe in this 1923 photo. On the left is the ranch barn. [Courtesy Oklahoma Historical Society, neg. #12255.

LEFT: The town and train station near the 101 Ranch were first called Bliss but were changed to Marland on April 8, 1922. A 1925 tag is on the car in foreground. [Courtesy Velma and Ray Falconer Collection.]

TOP: Fouquet's Racket and Grocery Store sprang up at Pond Creek right after the land run. It offered a wide variety of merchandise, including fresh bread, brooms, and shovels. [Courtesy Kansas State Historical Society.]

BOTTOM: Homesteaders gathered around the Rock Island Town Company at Pond Creek after the Strip run. Pond Creek lost its bid to keep the county seat. [Photo courtesy Kansas State Historical Society.]

Chapter Fifteen

Fighting Over the Spoils

The Big Counties Are Carved Up

IN RETROSPECT, one wonders why the government chose the run to open Oklahoma lands to settlement. In the Cherokee Strip especially, the method was cruel and unfair, even beyond individual suffering. Those who settled in the far western arid counties faced much more difficulty proving their claims and surviving for the required five years on their 160 acres than those who chose homesteads in the fertile eastern part of the Strip.

The land run method is attributed to President Grover Cleveland, who was first elected in 1884 and who was in office when the 1889 Oklahoma land run was planned. He was defeated in 1888 but returned to office in 1892 in time for the Cherokee Strip run.

The experience of four land runs finally brought about a wiser method, the lottery, in opening 13,000 acres of Plains Indian lands in 1901. A lottery for Strip lands would have prevented hardships, violence, and legal squabbles that lasted for years.

While the ordeal of the run was agonizing, life after that was as bad or worse.

With the fall came devastating prairie fires. The winter brought blizzards that covered dugouts and sod houses. In the spring came tornadoes raking across all sections of the Strip, and in the summer drought and blistering heat made life almost unbearable.

Women played a major role in keeping the destitute pioneers alive. They made the most of every facet of their environment. In the first days, kaffir corn was an important crop, and Margaret Nix of Ponca City recorded in her memoirs:

> We made kaffir cornbread, kaffir pancakes, kaffir hominy, turnip slaw and...sometimes we would manage to get hold of a little sorghum, and when we tired of it, we added an egg, some butter, cooked it awhile and made excellent spread for our bread. Meat was very scarce. When we had none, we browned a little sugar in the skillet, added lard and flour and milk or water, and made good gravy.[1]

Women in the Salt Plains manufactured their own salt. They put the soil from the plains in an iron kettle, covered it with water, and inserted a long-handled spoon. As the water boiled, the salt separated from the soil and settled in the spoon.[2]

Dugouts were lined with canned goods as women helped grow gardens and canned fruits and vegetables. There were no roads in the beginning and women drove wagons across country and through streams and rivers to buy material for making clothes for all the family. Men tilled the soil to grow cash crops, butchered hogs, and worked on other farms to help the family survive.

Counties Change

While individuals struggled to survive, they fussed over names of their counties, the location of county seats, and whether the two large counties, Woods and Woodward, were too large.

The question of county names was settled on November 6, 1894 as voters chose from suggestions by the Demo-crats, Republicans and Populists. Some county seat fights continued until statehood. In Kay County, Kildare was originally designated the seat, but after a group of Cherokees took their allotments there, the government moved the seat to Newkirk before the land run.[3] As stated in an earlier chapter, Newkirk fought off efforts by Blackwell and Ponca City and in 1912 finally was declared county seat.

The Grant County fight lasted until 1908, the year after statehood. The original county seat townsite was called Round Pond on a stream called Pond Creek but was moved four miles south of there and then became Pond Creek. Round Pond became Jefferson.

About 8,000 settlers swarmed into Pond Creek during the run. The town soon boasted a post office, established on September 29, 1893, a hotel, 12 law offices, two general stores, and several grocery stores.[4] It lacked one ingredient for success—a railroad station. The Rock Island depot was at Round Pond and the railroad refused to stop at Pond Creek.

A 1991 photo shows that little is left of Kildare in Kay County, which was at first designated as the county seat. When Cherokees took their land allotments near there, the government yanked the county seat away to put it at Newkirk. [Photo by author.]

Pond Creek boosters began a campaign of harassment against the railroad that included dynamiting bridges, placing obstructions on the tracks, tearing up tracks, and even sniping at railroad guards as trains passed through. All such tactics proved fruitless, but Pond Creek was able to remain as county seat until statehood.[5]

In the meantime, Medford had begun a series of legal maneuvers to take the county seat from Pond Creek. Pond Creek won an election held on May 16, 1899, but the courts voided the results because Oklahoma was still a territory and the county seat had been designated by the government. After statehood, Governor Charles N. Haskell ordered another election. Medford prevailed in this one and on June 9, 1908, Haskell proclaimed Medford the Grant County seat. On August 28, 1908 the state Supreme Court declared the election valid and Medford the legal county seat.[6]

Counties Are Carved Up

Of greater importance to the Strip was the realigning of county boundaries in 1907. The Enabling Act passed by Congress in 1906 provided for Oklahoma statehood and a constitutional convention. The convention met in Guthrie on November 20, 1906 in Guthrie and remained in session until July 7, 1907.

One of the great issues at the session was the question of county lines. Pressures were growing to divide the larger counties into smaller units. These included two in the Strip, Woods and Woodward. Charles N. Haskell and William H. Murray were largely responsible for the report adopted by the convention that carved up the two counties.[7]

Alfalfa and Major counties were created from the great "Empire of Woods." From the partition of Woodward County came Harper County, the northern part of Ellis County and the western part of

The Arkansas Daily Traveler predicted the big city of the Outlet would be Willow Springs in Kay County because its springs could furnish plenty of water for cattle and a city. But about all that was left a short time after the run were these bottling works. [Courtesy Newkirk Historical Community Museum.]

Woods County. Vigorous protests from Woodward and Woods counties went unheeded.

Alfalfa County was named for William H. (Alfalfa Bill) Murray and Cherokee was designated the county seat. Major County was named for John C. Major, a delegate to the convention, and

TOP: When Alfalfa County was carved from Woods County at statehood, Ingersoll had great hopes of becoming the county seat. It once had a bank, post office, several grain elevators and an attractive hotel, but it lost to Cherokee and eventually dwindled to a small settlement. [Courtesy Mary W. Erskine.]

BOTTOM: The original Grant County seat called Round Pond was near Jefferson, but was moved four miles south to Pond Creek. Jefferson was once a lively community with a railroad, but this 1991 photo shows the remnants of its abandoned city hall and elevator. [Photo by author.]

Fairview, the county seat, was named for its scenic location. Buffalo, the Harper county seat, was named for a nearby creek, and the county was named for Oscar G. Harper, a constitutional convention clerk.[8]

With counties all named, their boundaries defined, and county seats decided, the pioneers of the Cherokee Strip began in earnest to lay a lasting foundation for the land that would be home for them and their descendants.

TOP: Cherokee was originally three miles north of its present location. It was named Alfalfa County seat at statehood and has consistently been a leading center of alfalfa hay and livestock production and one of the state's top counties in agricultural cash receipts. [1991 photo by author.]

BOTTOM: Medford's water tower and courthouse are silhouetted in this 1991 photo, perhaps as symbols of its pride as Grant County seat, won at statehood from Pond Creek. [Photo by author.]

TOP: Caravans of as many as 34 wagons loaded with broom corn were seen often in Cherokee Strip towns. Good broom corn often brought $70 a ton. [Courtesy Oklahoma Historical Society, neg. #5445n.]
BOTTOM: In 1896, D. G. and Zada Harned acquired high tech McCormick equipment for harvesting wheat on their farm near Helena. [Courtesy Edith and Glenn Douglas.]

Chapter Sixteen

The Strip in Crisis

Farmers, Oil Men Fight to Survive

IN SOME RESPECTS, the Cherokee Strip has come full circle in its 100 years since the run. In the 1990s, as in the 1890s, the farmers were struggling to survive. After peaks of prosperity and growth, the Strip's economy was being threatened by severe problems in agricultural and oil production and a dramatic loss in population.

Great changes have come about in farming since the land run. The original settlers needed cash in a hurry to survive and to help pay off their land. Among the favorite early crops, especially in western Strip counties, were castor beans, broom corn and kaffir corn. Even into the early 1900s, wagons loaded with these crops came to markets in key Strip towns.

The beans were used to make castor oil, the laxative most pioneer children dreaded, and they could be used to produce a lubricant for certain types of machinery. The margin of profit was low and farmers soon switched to other crops, although some castor beans were being marketed as late as 1950.

Wagon trains carrying broom corn crowded into Woodward and Alva. This was also a good cash crop for a time but competition from Mexican producers and replacing of natural straw with synthetics brought an end to its production. Kaffir corn was largely replaced by higher grade sorghums and other crops after its early use.

Wheat Fields Increase

But the Strip farmers moved quickly to achieve their dream—to turn the vast land into waving wheat fields. By 1920, the earliest statistics, the Strip counties, including Harper and Ellis, produced 20,661,000 bushels of wheat of the state's total of 55,905,000. This was approximately 37 percent.[1]

By 1940 this percentage had grown to 42 percent. In 1990, the Strip counties were still producing more than 38 percent of the state's wheat, even with the diversification of crops and the increased production of wheat in southwestern, west central and central Oklahoma.[2]

Cherokee Strip counties also ranked high in other agricultural production compared to other Oklahoma counties. Alfalfa County in 1990 was a leader in alfalfa hay production. It and Woods County ranked high in livestock population, Woodward and Noble Counties were leaders in oat crops, Kay produced more than a half million bushels in grain sorghum, and along with Noble, Grant, Garfield, and Major, was a significant barley producer. In 1988, Strip counties brought in cash receipts of more than $35 million from agricultural products. Alfalfa County ranked second in the state.[3]

Farmers Suffer

These figures paint a glowing picture of agriculture in the Cherokee Strip, but they tell only part of the story. Many farmers were actually struggling for survival. They were at the mercy of the weather—victims at times of overly abundant rainfall, even flooding, and then prolonged droughts. Added to these

were problems of increased production costs, high interest rates, erratic government policies, and especially declining wheat prices. The plight of farmers throughout the nation has been such that the suicide rate increased markedly in the late 1980s.

Current studies show how these factors are changing farming both in the state and the Strip. The number of farms in the state decreased by more than 2,000 since 1985. This pattern was true in the Strip. In 1990, a survey showed that more than half of Oklahoma farmers were making more of their income from outside sources than on the farm. This became necessary to maintain a rural lifestyle.[4]

A significant number of farm and ranch operators in eastern Oklahoma were retired from other jobs. They became cattle producers with no acres in cropland. In the western area, including the Strip, crops continued to be the major source of income. One 1990 survey showed that a considerable number of

A familiar sight in Oklahoma during the oil crisis has been used oil field equipment for sale. This 1991 photo was taken at Cushing. [Photo by author.]

farmers was technically insolvent—that is, the amount of money they owed was greater than the value of their holdings.[5]

In the past it has been tradition for one or more sons to succeed their fathers in the Strip farm operations. This tradition declined as a future in farming became a great risk. The average age of the farm owner in Oklahoma in 1990 was 58.[6] The factors affecting Cherokee Strip agriculture were prevalent in many other farm areas and could eventually bring about a national crisis in agriculture.

The Glory Days of Oil

While the Cherokee Strip is generally known as cattle and wheat country, it experienced an exciting era of oil discoveries that began a few years after the land opening. Exploration for oil had been made as early as 1883, but it was not until 1911 that the first important discovery was made.

The man who opened the Strip oil era was Ernest W. Marland, who had for several years searched for oil in Pennsylvania, West Virginia, and Ohio.[7] He once struck oil while mining for coal in West Virginia and amassed a million dollars, but lost his fortune during the 1907 depression. In 1908 a nephew told him of the Cherokee Strip and suggested he explore there.[8]

Through the aid of Col. George Miller of the 101 Ranch, Marland obtained several leases on Ponca Indian land. His efforts resulted in eight dry holes before the ninth became a gusher in June 1911.[9] This was the beginning of the Ponca City field and it brought hordes of oil men into the area. Among names that would be associated with the oil history of the Strip were Thomas B. Slick and Bernard B. Jones, who opened the Drumright-Cushing field, Lew Wentz, Joshua S. Cosden and Herbert H. Champlin.

The intense exploration, largely in

Herbert H. Champlin was known largely for his oil interests but in 1900 he operated this lumber yard on the northeast corner of Enid's square. [Courtesy Darrel E. Keahey Collection.]

1916-17, led to new fields at Blackwell, Newkirk, Billings and Garber, and Tonkawa. The Garber field began in September 1917 with a 200-barrel a day well brought in by Sinclair Oil and Gas Company. It was one of the spectacular discoveries of that period and eventually produced more than 70,000 barrels of oil daily.[10]

Discovery at Three Sands

Of even greater magnitude was the Tonkawa Field brought in by a combination of producers, including Marland and Cosden, on June 30, 1921. The field was also known as Three Sands because the oil came from three principal sands called the Upper Hoover, Lower Hoover, and Tonkawa.

By April 1, 1921, the field had produced 675,000 barrels of oil and within two years it was reporting 112,112 barrels daily. The field also captured the attention of the petroleum industry because of its prolific natural gas production. By June 1923, royalties from the field were estimated at $100,000,000.[11]

With the vast oil production underway, Herbert H. Champlin took advantage of the situation by establishing a refinery at Enid. A hardware merchant and banker, Champlin financed considerable production in the field and was successful on a lease of his own. He set up pipelines to bring oil to his refinery from fields in Garber, Seminole, Tonkawa and even Oklahoma City.[12] The names of Champlin and Marland were on service stations throughout Oklahoma and beyond.

Oil Declines

The Strip oil fields followed a familiar pattern of reaching peak production in two or three years and then going into a decline. The Tonkawa field peaked in

The empty Zorba building on the north side of the Perry square is symbolic of business changes in the Cherokee Strip. T. E. Zorba founded the store in 1939 and it operated until 1987, attracting patrons from miles around. [Photo by author.]

1923 and then began a steady decline. Garber's highest production came in 1926 and then decreased rapidly.[13]

Only a few remnants exist of the exciting Strip oil days. Once oil derricks were so dense at Three Sands they appeared almost as trees in a forest. Today, only concrete foundations of business houses show up among the weeds. Marland's oil empire collapsed during the 1929 depression and his company was absorbed by Continental Oil Company.

The Continental Refinery, now known as Conoco Inc., purchased by DuPont in 1981, is still a mainstay of Ponca City's economy. One of the last giants to fall was the Champlin Refining Company in Enid. It closed in 1983. Individuals still explore for oil in the area, using new techniques in efforts to capture oil still in the ground, but the glory days of Strip oil are undoubtedly gone forever.

In 1973, decades after the demise of most major Oklahoma oil fields, another oil boom seemed in the making after Arab nations (Organization of Petroleum Exporting Countries) declared an embargo on oil shipments to the United States. An oil shortage and dramatic price increase sent oil explorers scurrying over the state to increase the domestic supply.

The search for oil and natural gas brought hundreds of oil workers into nearly all Cherokee Strip counties, particularly Garfield and Noble. Unfortunately for them, the Arabs rescinded their embargo and oil prices collapsed. Many explorers were left in dire financial straits with heavy equipment on hand and in debt. The collapse brought high unemployment among oil workers.

Many Cherokee Strip towns attribute their population losses shown in the 1990 census to the departure of these transient workers. The magnitude of the oil decline was emphasized by the Interstate Oil and Gas Compact Division in a report showing that 2,000 Oklahoma

Peace and quiet prevail in the area once known as Hell's Half Acre between the railroad tracks and Sixth Street in Perry. Behind these service establishments facing Cedar Street is a car lot. [Photo by author.]

wells with marginal production were closed down in 1990.

The oil crisis hurt farmers, too. Many lost oil royalties from their land that had provided them with funds to repair equipment and to pay on loans. For some, royalties were a margin of survival.

Hopes for revival of the oil industry were diminished further in 1991 as environmentalists sought to have oil exploration and production wastes classified as hazardous wastes and subject to federal control under the Resources Conservation and Recovery Act. And Bill Burks, chairman of the Oklahoma-Kansas Mid-Continent Oil and Gas Association, commented, "Unfortunately, in Oklahoma, the price for greater regulation and stricter environmental standards, even at the state level, will likely be fewer producing oil wells, less production, reduced revenues, and more unrecovered oil. The more requirements for protecting the environment that are put on oil and gas

wells, the more costly it is to operate them. More wells will become marginal or uneconomical and are plugged."[14]

The Population Shrinks

The population of the Strip just after the run was difficult to ascertain. Estimates of the number making the run came from witnesses or participants at the registration points and they varied by as much as 25,000 at some locations. If one accepted the maximum estimates at all points, the number would probably total 300,000. The generally accepted range is that 100,000 to 125,000 competed for claims that day.

The earliest reliable population figure of all Strip counties is 74,829, tabulated in February 1894.[15] For a time after that the population decreased as many settlers could not endure the hardships of living. A surge for immigration then

One of the major changes in Ponca City's business district during the Cherokee Strip crisis was the closing of Paris Furniture in 1989. The firm had operated in the 500 block of Grand Avenue since 1927. Ernest W. Marland built most of that block. [Photo by author.]

occurred in 1900 as Congress passed the Free Homes Act and decided after all not to charge for the Strip land.[16]

When statehood came in 1907, the total Strip population was 184,561, including all of Ellis County.[17] By 1910, smaller western counties had already reached a population peak and have been declining since. Others grew or remained fairly stable until the 1929 depression and the dust bowl, and then began a decline. A few counties such as Garfield, Kay, and Woodward increased in population until 1986 but have decreased mark-

edly since then, possibly because of the drastic drop in crude oil prices that year.[18]

Perhaps the most surprising figure from the 1990 preliminary census is that the Strip population was 188,210, just slightly above that at statehood. This figure includes all of Ellis County. Four counties in 1990 had total populations of fewer than 10,000, and two had fewer than 5,000.[19] The figures in the table below show the key years of population change.

Some community leaders have ques-

Rise and Decline of Population In Cherokee Strip Counties

County	1907	1910	1930	1986	1990
Alfalfa	16,070	18,138	15,228	6,900	6,416
Ellis	13,978	15,375	10,541	5,600	4,497
Garfield	28,300	33,050	45,588	62,900	56,735
Grant	17,638	18,760	14,150	6,500	5,689
Harper	8,089	8,189	7,761	4,700	4,063
Kay	24,757	26,999	50,186	52,200	48,056
Major	14,307	15,248	12,206	9,100	8,055
Noble	14,198	14,495	15,119	11,800	11,045
Pawnee	17,112	17,332	19,882	17,300	15,575
Woods	15,517	17,567	17,005	10,400	9,103
Woodward	14,595	16,592	15,844	21,800	18,976
Total	184,561	201,745	223,510	209,200	188,210

This table shows the population of Cherokee Strip counties at statehood and then when each county reached its peak and began to decline.

Population Changes in Cherokee Strip Towns

	1980	1990	Loss	Note
Alva	6,416	5,495	921	
Blackwell	8,400	7,538	862	
Cherokee	2,105	1,787	318	
Enid	50,363	45,309	5,054	
Fairview	3,370	2,936	434	
Newkirk	2,413	2,168	245	
Pawnee	1,688	2,197	509	a gain
Perry	5,796	4,978	818	
Ponca City	26,238	26,359	121	a gain
Tonkawa	3,524	3,127	397	
Woodward	13,610	12,340	1,270	

tioned the reliability of the 1990 census and perhaps justifiably. For instance, Pawnee showed a 500 increase in population, which not even its enthusiastic boosters believe. Other towns that showed losses were skeptical of the methodology employed in the census.

Towns Decline, Too

Except for Ponca City and Pawnee every major town in the Cherokee Strip has decreased in population since 1980, according to the preliminary 1990 census.

While these losses are significant, they are not unique to the Cherokee Strip. All across America, small towns and cities have been hurt by the migra-

tion from rural to urban areas, the difficulty of making a profit from farming, the increase of discount houses and shopping malls in nearby cities, and the departure of young people to areas where job opportunities exist.

Discount houses that sell merchandise at a price near what it cost an independent merchant to buy have been a major factor in the decline of main streets in the Strip and elsewhere. Empty buildings in many once-thriving communities are stark evidence of the impact of these cut-rate stores. The tax base of some small towns is being undermined by this trend, making it difficult for them to finance their city governments and schools.

Gone from most small town business

Orlando is on the line from which the land runs of 1889 and 1893 were made. Its population once reached 13,000, but about the only signs of life on its main street in 1991 were at a convenience store amid vacant buildings. [Photo by author.]

districts in 1990 were such stores as J. C. Penney Co., C. R. Anthony Co., Safeway, and home-owned general stores that once made the towns trading centers of their respective counties. These have been replaced by small specialty stores, and antique stores, or the buildings were still empty.

Yet, in spite of these many economic problems and population trends, leaders in the Cherokee Strip reflected confidence that a prosperous future lies ahead and they were busy trying to make this a reality.

TOP: Randolph Street on the north side of the square illustrates how Enid has beautified its business district with modernized store fronts, plants, and shrubbery. [Photo by author.]
BOTTOM: For years, Conoco Inc., has provided the base of Ponca City's economy with its nearly 4,000 employees. Conoco is now making its Research and Development Center (right) available for product testing and development to aid the city's drive for new industries. [Courtesy Conoco Inc.]

Chapter Seventeen

The Years Ahead

Cities Turn to Industry and Tourism

THE CENTENNIAL OBSERVANCE seemed to rekindle the pioneer spirit in the Cherokee Strip. Cities and towns were optimistic about the future and were taking steps to offset the losses caused by the agricultural and oil crises. Some had already achieved enough success to feel they were on the way to recovery. These steps included recruiting new industries, expanding present ones, tourism, revitalizing business districts, and creating activities that would bring people into town.

Air Base Helps Enid

An example was Enid. In 1990, the city government contracted with the Enid Development Coalition to promote economic development. Using a sales tax to finance the operation, the Coalition's mission was to retain existing industry and jobs, to seek new industry, and to support small businesses.[1]

Through working with the Coalition, one meat processing plant had been able to expand its operations space by 150,000 feet and estimated it would soon have 570 employees. An attractive brochure was sent to other industries telling of Enid's assets. These include three rail lines, a municipal airport, an available work force, and a high quality of life. At nearby Vance Air Force Base, 2,400 military and civilian personnel provided a strong base for the city's economy.[2] Another employee force of 800 operates the Enid State School for the developmentally disabled in Oklahoma.

A three-day Mid-America Summerfest sponsored by the Enid A.M. Ambucs started in 1986 and attracts 30,000 to 40,000 each year. In the fall, the annual Cherokee Strip celebration brings another mass of humanity. Enid's Cherokee Strip Conference Center, built in 1987, has attracted many conventions and short courses. A Higher Education Center was to begin in 1991 in downtown Enid. Four state universities, including Oklahoma State, were prepared to offer eight degree programs.

The city has begun a beautification program around the courthouse square. Store fronts have been modernized, planters and shrubbery line the streets, and efforts continued to bring high quality retail establishments to the area.

Ponca City Shows Gain

Ponca City was the only major city in the Cherokee Strip to show a population gain in 1990 even though Kay County experienced a substantial loss from 1986. In 1991, major expansion programs and an economic development plan were underway that could ensure the city's growth over the next decade.

Major projects included a Witco $20 million construction project on the south edge of Ponca City, a new 120,000 square feet store by Wal-Mart, a new K-Mart Store 90,000 square feet in size, and other projects involving several million dollars each.[3]

Conoco Inc. employs nearly 4,000 people. This provides a strong base for Ponca City's economy. In 1991, the company undertook a $900,000 program to beautify the outer edge of the refinery and another $9 million project to reconstruct a rewaxing unit that burned in May 1990.[4]

A new Economic Development Foundation worked to bring industrial ventures to town. The city and Conoco reached an agreement whereby some of the company's Research and Development Center space will be used for product testing and development. This project is concerned with products that have been developed by large corporations but which have never been promoted or marketed because they did not fit in well with the corporation's plans. The Foundation hopes small companies might take

Built in 1987, the Cherokee Conference Center is one of Enid's major economic assets. [Photo by author.]

these products and generate a profit. In some cases, inventors may have access to space.[5]

Ponca City is in the geographic center of what it calls an "aero triangle" of Tulsa, Oklahoma City, and Wichita. The Foundation has identified materials these air centers use and is recruiting companies that serve these aviation centers.

Other projects include a venture capital corporation to make capital available for small business equity capital, the promotion of 640 acres of Oklahoma School Land Commission as a regional industrial park, and a plan to provide capital at a reduced interest rate for manufacturing and processing industries. The Foundation has already identified 4,500 companies that it believes would find Ponca City an ideal industrial site.[6]

Blackwell Is Optimistic

Located just 15 miles south of the Kansas border on Interstate Highway 35, Blackwell's motto is "Blackwell Tops Oklahoma," and its community-wide theme for 1991 was "Optimism." The town Col. Andrew Jackson Blackwell founded a hundred years ago has been a busy place. It is in the rich Kay County wheat country and it shared in the major oil producing days of the 1920s. It once boasted the largest zinc smelter in the world.

Like most Cherokee Strip towns, it lost some transient population as oil exploration declined in the 1980s and the number of farms diminished. Its major loss, however, came in 1974 when Blackwell Zinc closed. Founded in 1916, the smelter once had 32 furnaces and at its peak employed about 2,000 people.

The 100 block of North Second Street in Blackwell was owned by Colonel Andrew Jackson Blackwell. His tin three-story hotel stood where the bank is located in this scene. [Photo by author.]

TOP: Alva senior citizens hope that the Bell Hotel, once one of the finest in northwest Oklahoma, can someday be converted into downtown apartments. An elegant showplace after it opened January 1, 1927, the Bell closed in the 1950s. It is located at Fifth Street and Barnes. [Photo by author.]
BOTTOM: The High Plains VoTech School, opened in 1984, has enhanced Woodward's reputation as a trade and educational center. [Photo by author.]

Blackwell has stabilized since that loss and is engaged in a vigorous campaign for industries and tourism as a base for its economy. Working together in 1991 were the Blackwell Industrial Authority, the chamber of commerce, and a number of city committees.

The smelter site had been cleared and converted to an industrial park. The primary targets of the Industrial Authority were manufacturers dealing in plastics, metal fabrication, warehouse/transportation, and food processing and packaging.[7] A special effort was being made to attract industries from states with high tax burdens. Blackwell leaders emphasized their city's affordable land costs, lower labor costs, tax benefits, a labor force, and employee training programs.[8]

The Cherokee Outlet Museum is a special tourist attraction, and the chamber of commerce joined with six other northern Oklahoma towns to promote tourism for the entire area. Community spirit was high in Blackwell in 1991 and optimism seemed more than just a slogan.

NOSU Grows in Alva

Alva has adopted a four-fold program to offset its agricultural and population losses. The city was enthusiastic as it prepared for the Centennial and optimistic that its plans for the future would succeed.

The town will give priority to supporting its existing assets, the most important of which is Northwestern Oklahoma State University (NOSU). The school has grown from a two-year program to a full-fledged university and of-

Woodward's recruiting activities have brought in such firms as this Mutual of Omaha operation with 60 employees. [Photo by author.]

fers several advanced degree programs. In 1991, its enrollment approached 2,000, and total full-time personnel numbered approximately 165.[9] The city is backing the university in its efforts to become an even broader reaching institution.

An industrial team at Alva is working for economic development. Its priority has been to help several small industries there build volume. One of the latter, the Kinzie Industries, was the first in Oklahoma to receive a grant under a new program of the Oklahoma Gas and Electric Company. A $10,000 award enabled Kinzie to provide high intensity furnaces that bake plastic parts used in aircraft. A second O. G. & E. grant was used to construct an addition to Alva's airport. The industrial team will seek other industries that lend themselves to that area.[10]

The team believes that Alva would be an ideal site for a state institution that would serve as a work camp for drug offenders. NOSU has specialists in social studies and law enforcement whose skills could be available for the camp.

A special part of Alva's promotion is tourism. For more than a quarter century, its Cherokee Strip Museum has been a major tourist attraction. This is especially true since 1975 when the Morton Share Trust presented the former Alva City Hospital to the Museum Association. Now the museum has 40 rooms that include displays not only of the

Charles Machine Works, Inc., at Perry, popularly known as Ditch Witch, is the realization of an American dream. It began as a blacksmith shop in 1902 by Carl Maltzahn. Now operated by his grandson, Edwin, it grosses $100 million in annual sales, its buildings cover 22 acres, and its nearly 800 employees provide the basis of Perry's economy. [Courtesy Charles Machine Works, Inc.]

Cherokee Strip and Oklahoma history, but of railroads, military history, and agriculture.

Alva is also in close range of the Great Salt Plains Lake, Alabaster Caverns, Little Sahara State Park, and the Burnham Archeological site, where remains have been discovered of the earliest signs of life in North America.

Woodward Gains Industries

Woodward, for many years the oil and agricultural center of far western Oklahoma, had the foresight to diversify its economy years ago. It has maintained its stability through the Cherokee Strip economic crisis better than some communities.

Although census figures show it lost more than 1,000 population from 1980 to 1990, many of those who left came during the oil and natural gas boom. Woodward has gained back much of this loss through its successful industrial development program, relying heavily on local mineral resources such as oil, gas, salt, and iodine.[11]

Among its major employers in 1991 were Terra International, a nitrogen fertilizer complex, with 80 employees; National Oilwell, with 135; USPIC, a hazardous waste disposal firm, with 78, and Western Iodine with 26.[12] The recruitment has brought in Trego Westwear with 75 employees, and Mutual of Omaha claims operation with 60 personnel. The High Plains Vo-Tech School established in 1984 is one of Woodward's greatest assets.[13]

Industrial recruitment was still going on there. A large industrial park was established four miles west of Woodward

Several thousand citizens gathered around the courthouse square in Perry on September 14, 1991, to watch a parade observing the 98th anniversary of the Cherokee Strip run. [Photo by author.]

near the municipal airport. A spur of the Santa Fe Railroad runs to the park.

Woodward's location on four major highways has caused it to be called Oklahoma's gateway to and from the West and has made it a trade center for far western Oklahoma counties. The location has also enhanced tourism. In town is the Plains Indians and Pioneers Museum and within a short distance are the Alabaster Caverns and Boiling Springs State Park.

Perry Planned Ahead

Once Hell's Half Acre in Perry was crowded with saloons, lawyers, and a wide assortment of businesses. Today all vestiges of the past are gone and a car lot takes up most of that area. But the town itself is very much alive.

Perry and Noble County are in the heart of the Oklahoma wheat country, and the area has also ranked high in barley, oat, and grain sorghum production. It has been a busy oil producing area since the 1920s. Thus, it suffered losses during the agricultural and oil crises. However, the city leaders were far-sighted enough to diversify the economy. Its payrolls in industry and related areas have been substantial enough to offset some of the farm and oil losses.

The major employer in Perry was Charles Machine Works, Inc., popularly known as Ditch Witch, with a work force of nearly 800. The Oklahoma Department of Transportation maintained an office in Perry with 125 employees. About 75 were employed at the Noble County courthouse. A half-dozen small industries operated in the area. Perry has

Pawnee has preserved many of its early buildings. With its annual Pow-Wow and Pawnee Bill Museum, it has become a favorite tourist site. [Photo by author.]

consistently had among the lowest unemployment rates in the state.[14]

At this writing, two committees were busy seeking to bolster Perry's economy with new industry. One was the Perry Development and Redevelopment Authority, and the other was a chamber of commerce development committee. One major project was to make available an 840-acre tract near the city airport as an industrial park.

Perry has several unusual assets for a small community that could tempt industry. It is just off Interstate Highway 35 that runs north and south and the Cimarron Turnpike and Highway 64 that run east and west. It has two railroad freight lines and an airport.

The efficiently operated Cherokee Strip museum just off I-35 has been a major tourist attraction for Perry. It has pictures and artifacts depicting the history of Oklahoma, the Cherokee Strip, and Noble County. Its picture collection is remarkable.

Pawnee Attracts Tourists

Smaller towns of the Cherokee Strip are also at work, although on a lesser scale, to offset their losses of main street businesses and population. Some of them have not been affected as much as the larger towns.

For instance, Pawnee's 1990 census is listed as 2,197, which would be a sizeable gain over that of 1980. A settlement has existed on that site since 1875 when the Pawnee Indian tribe was resettled from Nebraska. A post office was established in May 1876 for the Pawnee Indian Agency and it remained under that name until October 26, 1893.[15]

This central building is the hub for the large Pawnee Indian Agency complex at Pawnee. A post office existed here in 1876. [Photo by author.]

This historical background has made Pawnee a special tourist attraction. The Indian agency complex still operates on the south edge of the town. Toward the west is the Pawnee Bill Museum operated by the Oklahoma Historical Society. Many of Pawnee's old buildings have been preserved to add to the historical flavor. The annual Pawnee Bill Rodeo and the July Pow-Wow attract many visitors. In addition, the business leaders are working to bring in manufacturing industries to stimulate commerce.[16]

Tonkawa Has Stability

Tonkawa in Kay County is another of the Cherokee Strip's more stable communities. Although it has experienced losses through the agricultural and oil decline, its population has not changed much in the past 40 years. Its citizens are content to have it that way.

Important to Tonkawa's economy and community life is the Northern Oklahoma College, founded in 1901 as the University Preparatory School. In 1991, the two-year school had an enrollment of approximately 2,000 and a full-time work force of about 50.[17]

A high per cent of Tonkawa's population is retired. With the college students, this provides the community with a diverse age group. The town is just off Interstate Highway 35 and Highway 60, which makes it easy to get to larger cities. It is only 14 miles from Ponca City, and

In spite of the Cherokee Strip crises, Tonkawa in Kay County boasts a 75 percent survival rate for its businesses. In the background above is the Tonkawa mill, a vital factor in Tonkawa's economy during agricultural prosperity. [Photo by author.]

serves as a bedroom community for some Conoco Inc. workers.

Tonkawa has been able to fill most of its vacant buildings and is searching for new industries. A resurgence of agriculture would also be a great boon to the town. The school system's low student-teacher ratio has been a factor in attracting new residents.

Retirees Choose Fairview

Further west, Fairview has joined with the Major County Economic Development Corporation to secure new industries. Fairview is the county seat and trade center for the county. It is not built around a square since it became county seat at statehood when Major County was created. Before the land run, the government laid out all original county seat townsite on public squares.

The area actually gained in population from 1980 to 1986 but declined after the oil and agricultural crises. In spite of the decline, Fairview in 1991 still had about 30 oil related businesses, including the Cimarron Operating and Red Eagle Company, a trucking service company with about 150 employees.[18] Like most of the Strip Towns, the Fairview business district had several empty buildings, but unlike some others, it still had several chain stores, and its major automobile agencies were operating.

Retirees were becoming an important part of Fairview's economy. The town has moderate living costs, a good hospital and Fellowship Home. The latter is a nursing home with adjoining Fellowship Home Apartments for the elderly

These Fellowship Home apartments in Fairview adjacent to a nursing home have attracted elderly who want privacy and independence with care close by. Two additions have been built since the apartments opened in 1977. [Photo by author.]

who want privacy and independent living. Since Fairview is county seat and a trade center, it could maintain its economic stability if the Development Corporation is reasonably successful in its search for new industry.

These optimistic projections for the future come largely from the chambers of commerce or industrial development committees engaged in promoting industry in Cherokee Strip towns. The success some have already achieved, however, gives credence to their projections. They are taking advantage of a trend among industries to leave congested, high cost areas and to move to smaller communities. Their task will not be easy, since nearly every small town in America is competing for such industries.

Farm Outlook Dim

Most of the cities and towns in the Cherokee Strip hope that agriculture will make a comeback and will once again be a major factor in their economies. This may not be likely. Charles W. Anderson is a native of Enid in the Strip and has been involved in Oklahoma agricultural problems for years. In 1991, he was Assistant Commissioner of Agriculture in Oklahoma. He doubts that agriculture will ever be the same again.[19]

"We will never have a comeback to what we once had," he said. "The rural family farms as we have known them are a thing of the past. This is unfortunate because the roots of America came from well established rural people. But the prices in the world market and the demand of American consumers for lower food prices make it difficult for the small farmer to survive. Our consumers are spoiled. They readily accept higher prices on Japanese television or car prices, but if a gallon of milk goes up a few cents in

price, they complain loudly. Only 13 per cent of the dollar in America goes for food. In other nations the per cent is much higher and the closest to us is 33 per cent."

Anderson believes America will end up with fewer but bigger farms—with bigger operators buying out the smaller farms. He also sees the possibility of corporate farms such as exist on the West Coast. "Once we get corporate takeovers, food prices will go up," he said.

Hopefully, he added, the towns in the Cherokee Strip as well as elsewhere can have a mix of agriculture and industry. "And, people in these towns need to readjust. They need to reinstate their loyalties to home towns. They should buy at home rather than trying to save a few dollars by driving to out-of-town super markets and discount houses."

The Strip's Future

Considering all economic factors, the following projections seem likely in the Cherokee Strip for at least two decades;

1. Industry will replace agriculture as the economic base, but agriculture will still make an important contribution.

2. Tourism will increase through the combined efforts of all the key towns.

3. Population may remain relatively stable in larger towns, but more small villages will disappear as the number of family farms declines.

4. Buildings around the courthouse squares and on main streets will be occupied largely by specialty shops and offices.

5. The number of independent retailers will continue to decline.

These projections are for only the relatively near future and are subject to change because of wars, prolonged droughts, or a financial crisis in the national government.

It is doubtful that even the most imaginative mind could conceive what conditions may prevail in the Cherokee Strip in 2093, the bicentennial year. The pioneers of 1893 struggling to survive in dugouts and sod houses had scarcely begun to dream of indoor plumbing, electric lighting, and gravel roads. Any suggestions of radio, television, world-wide aviation networks, super highways, nuclear power, and modern medical techniques would have been mind-boggling to them.

Is it possible that all of these wondrous twentieth century developments will seem as primitive to the Cherokee Strip residents of 2093 as the sod houses, dugouts, and wagon trails of yesteryear seem to this generation?

With this question ends the bringing up to date of the Cherokee Strip history 160 years after it was created and 100 years after the great land run. Regardless of changes that come about in the vast land in the decades ahead, this story of the Cherokees, the run, and the founding of the Strip's towns should hold great fascination for all future generations.

The Eastman National Bank has been trimmed down to one story, but it is still on the corner of Seventh and Main Streets in Newkirk across from the courthouse. It started in 1893 as the Bank of Santa Fe. [Photo by author.]

ER BULLETIN. ARKANSAS CITY, KAN

IT IS OPENED !

THE GREAT CHEROKEE OUTLET

Is Now the Home of One Hundred
Thousand American Citizens.

An Empire With Countless Cities Build-
ed in a Day.

The Crack of the Carbine at High
Noon Gave the Signal to "Go."

Exciting Scenes From Places of Obser-
vation —A Lady Falls From Her
Horse.—Ed. Nicholson's Horse
Falls and, Being Disabled,
is Shot.—Nicholson Pur-
sues His Journey.

bore the appearance of the fabled
"deserted village." The boomers had
taken up the line of march and fully
one-half of the citizens had gone to
witness the great test of speed and
human endurance.

At the Santa Fe depot thousands
were assembled wondering and in-
quiring whether the facilities of the
road were equal to the great demand
that would be made upon its train service in a few hours. Good natured
crowds were at all of the livery stables,
begging, praying and swearing for
conveyances to the line. Men who
had never backed a horse were willing
to stake "their lives and sacred honor"
for a bucking broncho. Others wanted,
and would be satisfied with nothing
less than a cab and plug hatted driver.

The three roads leading to the territory were crowded with every conceivable vehicle. Men on horseback,
jumped fences and run at break-neck
peed through corn fields and plowed
ground. Hundreds, thousands of men
on foot with blankets and canteens at
their sides called to mind the days of
terrible war.

ON THE LINE.

At 7 o'clock the 100 foot strip designated by the department for camping
grounds for the homeseekers was packed with teams, wagons and a mass
of moving humanity. The farmer. the
banker, the merchant, the mechanic,
the cow boy and the tramp were fra-
ternizing as though they expected in
the near future, to become one family, subject to rules governing social
and business life in a new country.

A thousand or more teams filled the
road north of the Chilocco reservation.

The Arkansas Daily Traveler, September 16, 1893.

Chapter Eighteen

Reflections From One Hundred Years Ago

Some Eyewitness Recordings

HOW THOSE WHO LIVED through the famous Cherokee Strip Run experienced the great event is reflected on the following pages with news reports and illustrations taken from the September 16, 1893 edition of the *Arkansas City Daily Traveler* mixed with pages of the diary of a participant of the run.

On Thursday afternoon, August 31, 1893, two wagons carrying eight hopeful homesteaders left Berryville, Arkansas, to make the Cherokee Strip land run. Their number increased to 12 as four friends in two more wagons joined them in the Cherokee Nation.

By the time the caravan reached Stillwater on the southern border of the Strip on September 12, the pioneers had traveled nearly 600 miles in 28 days. They lived mostly on fish, birds, and fried squirrel. When they arrived, 2,500 men were already in line to register for the run, most of whom had slept there. By the time the Arkansans joined the line, it had grown to 4,000, and 13,000 had registered ahead of them.

Hugh Hanna of Berryville kept the daily diary of the journey found on the following pages. His observations, beginning on September 10, are presented here, taken from *The Carrol County* (Arkansas) *Historical Quarterly*, Summer of 1983.

The Berryville travelers were among the thousands disappointed in the race for land, as Sooners and others with faster horses beat them to claims they had hoped to win.

On to the Strip—A Diary

RICE, STIX & CO., ST. LOUIS, MO.   95

Sunday Sept 10

Eighteen Miles from Stillwater
Passed Ingalls in 5 miles
Some nice farms all
red Prairie land but
seems to produce well All
Kinds of crops growing and
all look Prosperous This
is a great hay country
camped on a creek one & half
miles east of Registering Bath
+ three miles from Still water
We are 1/4 miles south of Strip
Looks to be a fine prairie
as far as you can see
The prospect for a stranger
to get land is rather gloomy
The people have all The
land for miles all spatted

might w.

A company .   .bout 100
who seemed to have . proper appreciation of the situation raised their voices
in songs of doubtful melody

sold

starting .   .west
the Chillocoo . .erve and preven.
them from diverging to the west, so
that those starting from the state line

OLD RANGER---Got ther, and will hold his claim.

"This is the way I long have sought
And mourned because I found it not."

... . soon followed by a m^
... ^^... who ^

west of the reserve would have an
equal chan^^ ^^ ^hose who were di-
... ^^^

I am Eli but the Horse is Dennis

Flynn at once planned to get the floor and see if it was possible to choke off the resolution in that way. He at last succeeded in getting the floor and asked that the resolution be called up. The chairman of the committee on military affairs, Outhwaite, insisted that no one but the chairman of the committee or the acting chairman was able to call up the resolution. This point was submitted to the speaker, who concluded after some deliberation on the question, and after being prompted by Burrows, that as it was a privilege matter any member of the house had the right to call for its consideration.

This was the whole point won by ~nn, and at once the sparring over ~ution commenced. Flynn ob- ~ when he ended his remarks ~ng he reserved the re~ but On~ ~

Commissioner Lamoreaux said that no person had authority to charge fees for registration certificates, and he wanted to know if any employe of the department took fees.

Delegate Flynn of Oklahoma was then heard. He said that the Cherokee strip was under the jurisdiction of Oklahoma, and the sheriffs should have had charge of preserving the peace instead of the military. and, in sending the troops there, the government had perpetrated an outrage. He also stated that a Washington correspondent had told him (Mr. Flynn) that he had paid to register. Mr. Flynn then read letters charging the officials with fraud.

Mr. Hudson then made an argument for an investigation.

Commissioner Lamoreaux said that th~ ~ ~as an order allowing peo~ Indian lands ad~ ~ that ~

96 RICE, STIX & CO., ST. LOUIS, MO.

Monday Morning
Sept 11"
Decided to stay in camp
to day and see what the
prospects are for Registering
Dawson + Mc Kinnon
have gone to Stillwater
to get mail. To day is
twelve days since we saw
wife + babies,
Hugh + Harve went to Stillwater
And got one letter for Mc Kinnon
one for Harve + three for Hugh
All were glad to hear from
home and know all were
well

RICE, STIX & CO., ST. LOUIS, MO. 97

Tuesday Sept 12"
Went to Booth early but
found there was no chance
to get in to Register
About 250 men in line
Most of them had slept
in line in order to
hold their places,
We will have to take it
by turns Registering and
Keeping camp
Still Water had quite a
fire this evening
Burned Eight business
houses,

98   RICE, STIX & CO., ST. LOUIS, MO.

Wednesday Sept 13
John Sunday Emmit +
Harve went up to
Booth and got in line
before day   We took them
breakfast at 8; oclock
About 4000 men in
line   The Boys had
supper + bedding
Carried to them to night
and will sleep in line
to night
It looks like an army
to see so many men
in line + wagons Corrolled
together .
no one went to P.O. to day
Still water will to be
visited for mail
to morrow,

Leaving Arkansas City for the Strip, September 16th, 1893.

The Arkansas Daily Traveler, September 16, 1893.

Reflections From One Hundred Years Ago

RICE, STIX & CO., ST. LOUIS, MO.   99

Thursday Sept 14"
My self + Dutch John went
to the P.O. I got one letter
from wife + Babies.
The boys got the certificates
at 10 Oclock
McKinnon went in line
this evening
Reed Goodelock joined
our crowd
The prospects seemed worse
And the boys all home sick
John + I had fried Eggs
for supper

100   RICE, STIX & CO., ST. LOUIS, MO.

Friday Sept 15 ''
my self TheFreeman
+ John Woosley all went
up to the booth, went into
line at 10:30 and got through
at 3; 0 m.
We are all ready for the
run now,
Over 13000 people Registered
at this one booth,
We have about made up
our minds the whole strip
cut up into Town lots
would not make a claim
for each of the people waiting
To morrow is the day of days

RICE, STIX & CO., ST. LOUIS, MO. 101

Saturday Sept 16"

All up early getting ready
for the race loaded our
wagon and went to
Stillwater for supplies
met the other wagon up
on the line at 11:30.

The people on foot, wagons
buggies horse back and
every other way were formed
as far as you could see waiting
the signal. When the crowd started
we kept in the rear to see
the fun. one Lady seemed to
lead the way untill she
reached her claim

You could see men' staking
All over the prairie sticking
up their flags.

e who

Trains Entering the Strip Four Miles

By the hour
n, however,
f the plan to
succeeded in
rder given the
ng with those
est corner of
and prevent
he west, so
the state line

L. T. Bell, J. M. Jones, Geo. F. Rohr
and Guy Rohr. Their   are all
in excellent c
realize th

34 where the
to start from
12 o'clock

nth of Arkansas City, September 16th, 1893.

fleet footed horses were
At just two minutes of
oud of dust was seen to
he reser-
thous-
          n.

the shouts of their friends. Among
the number who starte   from
this   point   were   thr
two   of   wh m   r
pin fashion   d a m

102   RICE, STIX & CO., ST. LOUIS, MO.

we reached Black Bear
River at 2:30 and found
the bottoms full of people
some claims have several
men on them. All claim
to have got there first.
Here we stoped to rest and
feed. The other two wagons
came up but would not
stop to rest, just pulled
out for home. So our
crowd was reduced
we have camped here
for the night and look
over the country west
of here.
Reed Goudeloch and
Jim Felton stayed all
night with us,

RICE, STIX & CO., ST. LOUIS, MO.   108

Sunday. Sept 17;
This morning Mr Dawson.
took a notion to go home
we started west soon found
a goose pea patch and
gathered quite a lot,
Looked over some claims
and hunted some corners,
Have camped for dinner
and will probably stay here
to night, as Albert is trying
to buy out some "Sooners".
The wind is blowing so hard
Getting cloudy and looks like
rain for the first time since
we have been out,
What a lonely Sunday
in a country where there
is plenty of people but not
a house

The Rush for Town Lots at Willow Springs.

The Arkansas Daily Traveler, September 16, 1893.

104   RICE, STIX & CO., ST. LOUIS, MO.

Monday Sept 18"
Spent the morning
in trying to locate
Corners and figuring
on buying out some
claims, Failed to
trade and struck the
road west went about
10 miles in to the Osage
nation, Eat dinner on the
Black Bear, Held a
Consultation, and decided
to pull in the direction
of Arkansaw,
Came to the old Ranch
ford and camped,
Have not saw a house
for three days,

cents in payment for the hay He also told of the soldiers shooting E. N. Smith's horse in the state.

Col. Heyl then went and called on William Kilpatrick and secured his testimony.

He stated he was approached by a man, unknown. who told him he could get registered by tipping the soldiers. The man charged $1 and told him to give the soldier 50 cents. He was registered but in the excitement did not give the soldier his tip.

WHITEWASHED.

CONGRESS REFUSES TO INVES-TIGATE.

The Killing of Hill by one of the Soldiers on Sept 16.

Delegate Flynn is Making a Manly Fight for an Investigation.

But All to no Purpose—The War Department Will Take Such Steps as it sees fit, Which will Result in Nothing.

Whitewashed.

WASHINGTON, Sept. 30.—Despite the agreement yesterday to call up the Flynn resolution of inquiry into the murder of Hill, at Arkansas City, by a soldier on the 16th inst., which was entered into by both sides, it was decided this morning by the democrats to leave the resolution before the house and let the secretary of war act in the matter as he might desire.

When this became known Delegate

An Investigation.—Commissioner Lamoreaux Says no

Orders were Issued Permitting Persons to go Through "Indian" Reservations.

Delegate Flynn Says the Strip Was Under the Jurisdiction of Oklahoma, and the Sending of United States Troops Was an Outrage.

The Strip Frauds.

A General Demand for an Investigation.

WASHINGTON, Oct. 7.—The house committee on public lands held a special meeting yesterday to hear Mr. Hudson of Kansas upon the resolution he had introduced asking that a committee be appointed to investigate the charges against the civil and military authorities for alleged outrages in the opening of the Cherokee outlet. Commissioner Lamoreaux of the general land office and Chief Clerk Jacobs, the latter being one of the officers sent by the department to assist in the opening, were interested listeners.

Mr. Hudson said that he knew from reliable authority that persons had been allowed to enter the lands opened from the east side, getting advantage over other intending settlers. Certain men were responsible for this, and it was due to the department that an investigation be had. He said that he had proof that John R Hill of New Jersey was killed by the soldiers under the order of Lieutenant Caldwell.

Mr. Hudson read newspaper articles, in which charges were made of the sale and purchase of registration certificates with the knowledge and connivance of the officials. The charges were mostly of a general nature.

BLANKSTIX & CO., ST. LOUIS, MO. 105

Tuesday Sept 19"
Trailed down Black Bear
to Pawnee Agency Reached this
place at noon, and looked
over the new town, to be
the county site
Came to Arkensaw River
and camped.
C. L. Glines & Frank
Huntington of Harrison
Camped with us
    32 miles drive

Francis Marion (Bud) Dawson was among the pioneers whose experiences are described in this diary. Dawson was the great grandfather of Jack Allred, who painted the cover picture for this book. [Tintype courtesy Jack Allred]

List of Supplies Used on Trip

Sugar	$ .50
Bake Powder	.15
Coffee	.25
Bread	.50
Onions	.60
Bacon	2.00
Flour & etc. at Stillwell	1.00

Notes

Specific documentation is included for all chapters dealing with general Cherokee Strip history. Because fewer sources were used for the settling of individual towns, only bibliographies are included for those chapters, 7 through 14.

Chapter One

[1]Duane H. King, *The Cherokee Indian Nation- A Troubled History,*(University of Tennessee Press, 1979), 10-11.

[2]Earl Boyd Pierce and Rennard Strickland, *The Cherokee People,*(Phoenix: Indian Tribal Series, 1973), 12.

[3]Muriel H. Wright, *The Five Civilized Tribes,*(Norman: University of Oklahoma Press, 1951), 6.

[4] W. R. Smith, *The Story of the Cherokees,*(Cleveland: The Church of God Publishing House, 1928), 30-60.

[5]Ibid, 84-85.

[6]James Mooney, *Myths of the Cherokee Nation.*19th Annual Report of the Bureau of American Ethnology to the Smithsonian Institution - 1897-1898, Government Printing Office, 1900. Reprinted 1970 by the Scholarly Press, St. Clair Shores, Michigan; also W. R. Smith, *The Story of the Cherokees,*(Cleveland: The Church of God Publishing House, 1928), 85.

[7]Anthony F. Rice, "The Opening of the Cherokee Outlet, Oklahoma" (Typescript, Oklahoma Historical Society).

[8]Victor E. Harlow, *Oklahoma*(Oklahoma City, Harlow Publishing Company, 1949). 80.

[9]Ibid, 81.

[10]Ibid, 100-101.

[11]Edward Everett Dale, "The Cherokee Strip Live Stock Association," *Chronicles of Oklahoma,*V (March, 1927), 58.

[12]Harlow, 102.

[13]Harlow, 132.

[14]Ibid.

[15]Ibid.

[16]Leola Selman Beeson, "Homes of Distinguished Cherokees," *Chronicles of Oklahoma,*XI (September 1933), 929.

[17]William George Snodgrass, "A History of the Cherokee Strip," (Unpublished Ed.D. Thesis, Oklahoma State University, 1972), 6.

Chapter Two

[1]Edwin C. McReynolds, *Oklahoma, The Story of its Past and Present,*(Norman: University of Oklahoma Press, 1977), 91-92.

[2]Grant Foreman, *Indian Removal,*(Norman: University of Oklahoma Press, 1932), 286-287.

[3]Ibid.

[4]Ibid, 299.

[5]Ibid, 299-312.

[6]Ibid, 310; also Grace Steele Woodward, *The Cherokees,*(Norman: University of Oklahoma Press, 1963), 217

[7]Harlow, *Oklahoma,*147; Woodward, *The Cherokees,*224-225; Wright, *A Guide to the Indian Tribes of Oklahoma,*11.

[8]Wright, 12; Harlow, 148-149.

[9]Harlow, 150; Wright, 13.

[10]Harlow, 150.

[11]Wright, 12.

[12]D. E. Newsom, *Kicking Bird and the Birth of Oklahoma,*(Perkins: Evans Publications, 1983), pp. 28-31.

[13]Ibid.

Chapter Three

[1] Joe B. Milam, "The Opening of the Cherokee Outlet," *Chronicles of Oklahoma,* IX (December 1931), 454.

[2] Ibid, 454-455.

[3] Harlow, *Oklahoma,* 240.

[4] Ibid.

[5] Ibid, 240-241.

[6] Ibid.

[7] Milam, 209.

[8] Edward Everett Dale, "The Cherokee Strip Live Stock Association," *Chronicles of Oklahoma* V (March, 1927), 61.

[9] Milam, 269.

[10] Dale, 58.

[11] Milam, 270; Dale, 66-67.

[12] Dale, 67.

[13] Harlow, 242-243.

Chapter Four

[1] Eugene Couch, "One Pioneer Family," William L. and Cynthia E. Couch," Typescript in possession of author, 13.

[2] D. E. Newsom, *Kicking Bird and the Birth of Oklahoma, A Biography of Milton W. Reynolds,* (Perkins: Evans Publications, 1983). 73-74.

[3] Harlow, *Oklahoma,* 245.

[4] Snodgrass, *A History of the Cherokee Outlet,* 26-28.

[5] Carl Coke Rister, *Land Hunger,* (Norman: University of Oklahoma Press, 1942), 184.

[6] D. Earl Newsom, *Stillwater, One Hundred Years of Memories, A Pictorial History,* (Norfolk: The Donning Company, 1989), 42; also Basil Berlin Chapman, *The Founding of Stillwater,* (Oklahoma City: Times-Journal Publishing Co., 1948), 8.

Chapter Five

[1] *Perkins Bee,* September 8, 1893.

[2] Joe B. Milam, "The Opening of the Cherokee Outlet," *Chronicles of Oklahoma,* IX (December 1931), 456-275.

[3] Edward Everett Dale, "The Cherokee Strip Live Stock Association," *Chronicles of Oklahoma,* V (March 1927), 58.

[4] Milam, 455.

[5] Milam, 456.

[6] George Rainey, *The Cherokee Strip* (Guthrie: Co-operative Publishing Co., 1933), 266-317.

[7] Milam, 458.

[8] *Perkins Bee,* September 8, 1893.

[9] Ibid.

[10] William George Snodgrass, "A History of the Cherokee Strip," (Unpublished Ed.D. Thesis, Oklahoma State University, 1972), 32.

[11] *Perkins Bee,* September 8, 1893.

[12] Ibid.

[13] Ibid.

Chapter Six

[1] Joe B. Milam, "The Opening of the Cherokee Strip," *Chronicles of Oklahoma,* IX (December 1931), 461.

[2] Milam, *Chronicles of Oklahoma,* IX, (September 1931), 284.

[3] Clyde E. Muchmore, "I Saw the Run," (Ponca City: *The Last Run, Kay County, Oklahoma, 1893,* Courier Printing Company, 1934), 120.

[4] Ibid.

[5] Snodgrass, *A History of the Cherokee Outlet,* 35; also Rainey, *The Cherokee Strip,* 273.

[6] Basil Berlin Chapman, *The Founding of Stillwater,* (Oklahoma City: Times-Journal Publishing Company, 1948), 179.

[7] Lerona Rosemond Morris, *Oklahoma, Yesterday, and Tomorrow,* (Guthrie: Cooperative Publishing Co., 1930), 431-432.

[8] Milam, *Chronicles of Oklahoma,* IX, 473.

[9] Ibid, 475.

[10] Leona (Mrs. F. D.) Foutz, "Out of the Wind and Dust," *The Last Run,* 38.

[11] Milam, 285-467.

[12] *Perkins Bee,* September 8, 1893; Milam, 470.

[13] B. L. Long, "Memoirs of the Opening of the Cherokee Strip," *The Last Run,* 196.

[14] Milam, 467.

[15] *The Hennessey Clipper,* September 14, 1961.

[16] Milam, 278.

[17]Milam, 474.

[18]Muchmore, *The Last Run,*121; Rainey, *The Cherokee Strip,*277.

[19]Long, *The Last Run,*196-197.

[20]Anthony F. Rice, "The Opening of the Cherokee Outlet, Oklahoma," Typescript, Oklahoma Historical Society.

[21]Ibid, 5.

[22]*The Hennessey Clipper,*Sept. 14, 1961.

[23]S. Bee Crawford, "My Race, Council Grove Crawford," *The Last Run,*64.

[24]*Ponca City News,*Sept. 15, 1968.

[25]Milam, 469.

[26]*The Last Run,*35.

[27]Ibid, 27.

[28]Louis Seymour Barnes, "The Founding of Ponca City," *Chronicles of Oklahoma,*XXXV (Summer 1957) 156-157.

Chapter Seven (Bibliography)

Alva Centennial Commission, *Glimpses of the Past, Early Postcard View of Alva, Oklahoma,*(Alva: News-gram, 1987.

*Alva Pioneer.*Souvenir Edition, January 1, 1904.

*Alva Review-Courier,*July 29, 1936.

L. Edward Carter, *The Story of Oklahoma Newspapers,*(Oklahoma City: Western Heritage Books, Inc., 1984.

Mrs. Jack Erskine, interview May 21, 1991.

Pioneer Footprints Across Woods County,(Alva: Cherokee Strip Volunteer League, 1976).

Lerona Richmond Morris, *Oklahoma Yesterday, Today and Tomorrow,* (Guthrie: Co-op Publishing, 1930)

Seekers of Oklahoma Heritage Association, *Alva, Oklahoma, The First 100 Years,*(Curtis Media Corporation, 1987).

Ron Seamon, interview, January 24, 1990.

George H. Shirk, *Oklahoma Place Names,*Norman: University of Oklahoma Press, 1965).

William George Snodgrass, "A History of the Cherokee Strip," (Unpublished Thesis, Oklahoma State University, 1972).

Chapter Eight (Bibliography)

*Blackwell Rock Record,*Oct. 5, 1893-Dec. 26, 1895.

*Blackwell Times,*Nov. 1, 1893-Feb. 2, 1894.

Marijane Boone, *Newkirk and Kay County,*(Ponca City: Skinner & Sons, 1968).

Homer S. Chambers, *The Enduring Rock. History and Reminiscences of Blackwell and the Cherokee Strip, (Blackwell: Blackwell Publications, Inc., 1954).*

George H. Shirk, *Oklahoma Places Names,*(Norman: University of Oklahoma Press, 1989).

Chapter Nine (Bibliography)

*Enid Eagle,*Aug. 29, 1909.

*Enid Morning News,*Sept. 24, 1961.

Kent Ruth, Oklahoma, *A Guide to the Sooner State,*(Norman: University of Oklahoma Press, 1957).

William George Snodgrass, "A History of the Cherokee Strip," (Unpublished Ed.D. Thesis, Oklahoma State University, 1972).

Velma Troxel, Jayne and Stella Campbell Rockwell, *O County Faces and Places,*(Enid: Harold Allen, Publisher, 1968).

Alfred Tennyson, *Tennyson Poems & Plays,*(London: University of Oxford Press, 1973).

Chapter Ten (Bibliography)

Marijane Boone, *Newkirk and Kay County,*(Ponca City: Skinner & Sons, Printers 1968).

Daughters of the American Revolution, *The Last Run,*(Ponca City: 1970)

*Ponca City News,*Sept. 15, 1968.

Chapter Eleven (Bibliography)

Fred E. Beers, *The First Generation, A Half Century of Pioneering in Perry, Oklahoma*(Stillwater: The Oklahoma Legacy Series, 1991).

Robert E. Cunningham, *Perry, Pride of the Prairie,*(Stillwater: Frontier Printers, n.d.).

E. W. Jones, *Early Day History of Perry, Oklahoma*(Perry: 1931).

Ethel Katherine Knox, "The Beginning of Perry, Oklahoma," (Unpublished MA Thesis, Oklahoma A. and M. College, 1938).

Noble County Genealogy Society, *History of Noble County, Oklahoma,*(Saline, Michigan: McNaughton & Gunn, Inc., 1987).

William George Snodgrass, "A History of the Cherokee Strip," (Unpublished Ed.D. Thesis, Oklahoma State University, 1972).

Chapter Twelve [Bibliography]

Louis Seymour Barnes, "The Founding of Ponca City," *Chronicles of Oklahoma*, XXV (Summer 1957).

Daughters of the American Revolution, *The Last Run*, (Ponca City, 3rd ed., 1970).

Ponca City News, Sept. 15, 1968.

Kent Ruth, *Oklahoma—A Guide to the Sooner State*, (Norman: University of Oklahoma Press, 1957).

George H. Shirk, *Oklahoma Place Names*, (Norman: University of Oklahoma Press, 1965).

William George Snodgrass, "A History of the Cherokee Strip," (Unpublished Ed.D. Thesis, Oklahoma State University, 1972).

Chapter Thirteen [Bibliography]

Louise B. James, *Below Devil's Gap - The Story of Woodward County,*(Perkins: Evans Publications, 1984.

Ralph E. Randels, "The Homesteader and the Development of Woodward County," *Chronicles of Oklahoma*,XVII, 1939.

George H. Shirk, *Oklahoma Place Names,*(Norman: University of Oklahoma Press, 1965).

Woodward *Advocate,*September 23, 1893-November 23, 1894,

Woodward County Pioneer Families Before 1915(Woodward: Plains Indians and Pioneer Historical Foundation, 1975).

Chapter Fourteen [Bibliography]

Fred S. Barde Collection, "History - The 101 Ranch," Oklahoma Historical Society

Charles Lane Callen, "The Story of the Great 101 Ranch," *Oklahoma Yesterday, Today, and Tomorrow,*(Guthrie: Cooperative Publishing Co., 1930).

Ellsworth Collings, *The 101 Ranch,*(Norman: University of Oklahoma Press, 1971).

Daughters of the American Revolution, *The Last Run,*(Ponca City: 1970).

*Ponca City News,*September 15, 1968.

Chapter Fifteen

[1]Daughters of the American Revolution, *The Last Run,*(Ponca City, 3rd ed., 1970), 36.

[2]Ibid.

[3]Joe B. Milam, "The Opening of the Cherokee Outlet," (Unpublished Master's Thesis, Oklahoma State University, 1931), 45-46.

[4]William George Snodgrass, "A History of the Cherokee Strip," (Unpublished Ed.D. Thesis, Oklahoma State University, 1972), 81-82.

[5]Ibid.

[6]George Rainey, *The Cherokee Strip,*(Guthrie: Cooperative Publishing Co., 1933), 484-487.

[7]Victor E. Harlow, *Oklahoma,*(Oklahoma City: Harlow Publishing Co., 1949), 308-314.

[8]George E. Shirk, *Oklahoma Place Names,*(Norman: University of Oklahoma Press, 1965), 6, 33, 86, 109, 153.

Chapter Sixteen

[1]Oklahoma Statistical Service, Oklahoma Department of Agriculture.

[2]Ibid.

[3]Oklahoma Department of Agriculture, *Oklahoma Agricultural Statistics, 1989,*83.

[4]Ibid;. 98, 99.

[5]Ibid.

[6]Ibid.

[7]William George Snodgrass, "A History of the Cherokee Strip," (Unpublished Ed.D. Thesis, Oklahoma State University, 1972). 125, 126; Kenny Franks, Paul F. Lambert, and Carl N. Tyson, *Early Oklahoma Oil, A Photographic History, 1859-1936,*Ibid College Station: Texas A. & M. University Press, 1981), 145, 146.

[8]Snodgrass, 125.

[9]Franks, Lambert and Tyson, 146.

[10]Carl Coke Rister, Oil! *Titan of the Southwest.*(Norman: University of Oklahoma Press, 1949), 139-140.

[11]Ibid:.203.

[12]Ibid,.204;.

[13]Ibid,;. 410.

[14]*Fairview Republican,*Aug. 22, 1991.

[15]Snodgrass,. 230.

[16]Victor E. Harlow, *Oklahoma,*(Oklahoma City: Harlow Publishing Co., 1949), 272.

[17]State Department of Libraries, *Directory of Oklahoma,*376-535; U. S. Census, 1960-1990.

[18]Ibid.

[19]U. S. Census, 1990.

Chapter Seventeen

[1]Tom Sailors, Jr., President, Enid Development Coalition, interview with author March 6, 1991; Greater Enid Chamber of Commerce.

[2]Ibid.

[3]*Ponca City News,*April 16, 1991.

[4]Ibid.

[5]Bill Clifford, Director, Economic Development Foundation, Inc., Ponca City Chamber of Commerce, Interview with author June 6, 1991.

[6]Ibid.

[7]Three-Year Marketing Plan, Blackwell Industrial Authority, Joe Hodges, Director.

[8]Annual Marketing Goals, 1991-1992, Blackwell Industrial Authority.

[9]Public Information Office, Northwestern Oklahoma State University.

[10]Richard Ryerson, member, Woods County Industrial Authority and past president, Alva Industrial Team, telephone interview with author, July 20, 1991.

[11]Charlene Murdock, President, Woodward Chamber of Commerce, telephone interview with author, August 8, 1991.

[12]Ibid.

[13]Ibid.

[14]Roy E. Morris, Chairman, Perry Development and Redevelopment Authority, interview with author, August 6, 1991.

[15]George Shirk, *Oklahoma Place Names,*(Norman: University of Oklahoma Press, 1965), 187.

[16]Darrell Gambill, Manager, Pawnee Chamber of Commerce, interview with author, August 13, 1991.

[17]Public Information Office, Northern Oklahoma College, telephone interview, July 26, 1991.

[18]Bonnie Adamson, manager, Fairview Chamber of Commerce, telephone interview August 14, 1991.

[19]Charles W. Anderson, Assistant Commissioner of Agriculture, Oklahoma Department of Agriculture, telephone interview August 20, 1991.

Index

A

Aldrich, E. C.: 50.
Alfalfa County: 125, 130, 135.
Alva: 31, 45-47, 129, 135, 143, 144, 145.
Anderson, Charles W.: 150.
Arkansas City, Kansas: 30, 37, 40, 47.

B

Barnes, Burton S.: 96, 97, 99.
Beegle, Andy: 54.
Bell, John Adair: 6.
Benn, Robert and Zelah: 108.
Bickel, H. M.: 51.
Blackwell: 58-67, 132, 135, 141, 143.
Blackwell, Andrew Jackson: 58, 59, 60, 63, 64, 66, 67, 141.
Boatman, Zachariah: 51, 52.
Boomers: 22, 25, 26, 27.
Boudinot, Elias: 6, 7, 10, 14, 23.
Boudinot, Elias C.: 14, 22, 24, 25.
Brogan, John: 92.
Bryan, William Jennings: 111, 116.
Buffalo: 127.
Burks, Bill: 134.
Bushyhead, Dennis: 20, 27.

C

Caldwell, Kansas: 17, 18, 19, 30, 37, 40, 107.
Capron: 50.
Carpenter, Charles C.: 25.
Champlin, Herbert H.: 131, 132.
Charles Machine Works: 93, 144.
Cherokee: 127, 135.

Cherokee Advocate: 12.
Cherokee Indians,
    origin and early history: 1-7;
    Trail of Tears: 9, 10;
    new nation: 11;
    Civil War: 12, 13;
    Treaty of 1866: 14;
    sale of the Outlet: 28.
Cherokee Outlet/Strip,
    creation of: 1, 3, 5, 6, 7;
    Treaty of 1866: 14;
    movement of other tribes into: 16;
    cattle drives: 17-20;
    Boomers invade: 23, 25;
    lease to Live Stock Association: 20;
    sale to government: 28;
    preparing for opening: 29-33;
    the 1893 land run: 35-47;
    naming of counties: 124;
    realigning county boundaries: 124, 127;
    oil and agriculture decline: 130-134;
    population decline: 134, 135;
    outlook for future: 150.
Cherokee Strip: 1, 3 (see also Cherokee Outlet/Strip).
Cherokee Strip Live Stock Association: 19, 20, 27, 28, 29.
Chick, William and Amanda: 50.
Childers, Ed: 111.
Civil War: 12, 13, 23.
Clarke, Fred C.: 120.
Cleveland, Grover: 26, 29, 59, 74, 123.
Conoco Inc.: 133, 138, 140.
Cooley, D. N.: 14.
Cox, Joseph H.: 107.
Crawford, Council G.: 44.
Couch, William L.: 26, 50.
Cronkwright, W. G.: 99.
Cross: 97, 98, 99, 101.

D

Dalton, J. W.: 99.
Dean, Jerry R.: 108.
Ditch Witch: (see Charles Machine Works).
Dragging Canoe: 4.
Dwight Mission: 12.

E

Ellis County: 125, 129, 135.
Enid: 31, 44, 68-75, 133, 135, 139, 140.
Evans, Billy: 101.

F

Fairview: 127, 135, 149.
Fort Smith Council: 14, 24.
Foster, Judge Cassius G.: 26.

G

Galbraith, Al: 52.
Garfield County: 30, 135.
Gillett, Preston: 41.
Grant County: 30, 125, 130, 135.

H

Hale, William B.: 112.
Hall, C. M.: 112.
Harned, D. G. and Zada: 47, 128.
Harper County: 125, 130, 135.
Harper, Oscar G.: 127.
Haskell, Charles N.: 125.
Hatfield, W. F.: 54.
Hennessey: 29, 69.
Houston, Temple: 107, 108.
Hudson, Clark: 54.
Hunnewell, Kansas: 30, 42, 61, 63, 107.

I

Indian Territory: 6, 15.

J

Jackson, Andrew: 5, 6.
Jennings, Ed: 107.
Johnson, S. L.: 49.
Jones, Bernard B.: 131.
Jones, David W.: 106.
Jones, E. W.: 93.

K

Katy Railroad: 24.
Kay County: 30, 97, 130, 135.
Kildore: 124.
Kiowa, Kansas: 30, 34, 37, 49, 53.
Kokernut, Lee: 116.

L

Lamoreaux, S. L.: 81.
Laune, Sidney B.: 108.
Little, W. D.: 94.
Lorton, Otis: 37.
Love, Jack: 107.
Lovely Purchase: 5.
Long, B. L.: 40.

M

Major County: 125, 126, 135.
Marland, Ernest W.: 102, 119, 131.
Martinson, Peter: 107.
McKenzie, Dr. Henry: 70.
Medford: 125, 127.
Miller, George Lee: 114, 116, 118, 120, 131.
Miller, George W.: 115, 116, 117, 118.
Miller, Joe C.: 114, 115, 118.
Miller, Mollie: 114, 117.
Miller, Zachary T. (Zack): 114, 116, 117, 118, 120, 121.
Missouria Indians: 16.
Moore, John C.: 73, 74.
Mooney, James: 4.
Muchmore, Clyde E.: 35.
Murray, William H.: 125.

N

New Echota Treaty: 1, 6, 7, 23.
Newkirk: 31, 80-86, 97, 124, 132, 135, 151.
Nix, Margaret: 123.
Noble County: 30, 90, 130, 135, 146.
Noble, John W.: 90.

O

Oklahoma Bill: 26.
Oklahoma War Chief: 25.
Oklahoma Land Rush, 1889: 27.
101 Ranch: 114-121.
Orlando: 29, 37, 40, 42, 89, 107.
Otoe Indians: 16.

P

Parsons *Sun*: 24.
Parker, E. S.: 64.
Patterson, Robert M.: 71.
Pawnee: 135, 136, 146, 147.
Pawnee Indians: 16, 29.
Payne, David L.: 22, 25, 26.
Perry: 88-95, 135, 146, 147.
Perry, J. A.: 90.
Ponca City: 44, 45, 101-104, 135, 136, 140, 141.
Ponca Indians: 16, 116.
Pond Creek: 31, 124, 125.

R

Removal Bill: 6.
Renfrow, William C.: 73, 81.
Reynolds, Milton W. (Kicking Bird): 24.
Ridge, John: 6, 10, 11.
Ridge, Major: 6, 10, 11.
Rock Falls: 25.
Rock Island: 42, 70, 73, 74, 124.
Ross, A. J.: 54.
Ross, John: 7, 9, 11, 12, 14.
Round Pond: 124.

S

Schaeffer, Anton: 51, 52.
Sequoyah: 4, 5.
Semands, F. P., Rev.: 53.
Slick, Tom: 131.
Smith, Hoke: 30, 31, 40, 112.
Springer, William M.: 26.
Starr, James: 6.
Sooners: 31, 36, 46, 49.
Stillwater: 26, 29, 36, 107.
Swartz, Rev. B. C.: 82.
Swineford, Alfred P.: 32, 111.

T

Tahlequah: 8, 12, 20.
Tanner, Stephen B.: 50.
Taylor, L. H.: 52.
Thomas, A. M.: 83.
Three Sands: 132.
Tonkawa Field: (see Three Sands).
Tonkawa: 135, 148, 149.
Tonkawa Indians: 16, 29.
Trail of Tears: 9, 10.
Treaties of 1866: 14, 16, 23.

U

Unassigned Lands: 24, 26, 27.

W

Watchorn, Robert: 119.
Watie, Stand: 6, 10, 13.
Webb, William: 51.
Wentz, Lew H.: 102, 131.
Wharton, Lon: 94.
White Eagle: 117, 118.
Wiggins, W. H.: 49, 52.
Wilkinson, W. W.: 51.
Wood, Sam N.: 54.
Woods County: 30, 49, 125, 126, 130, 135, 143, 145, 146.
Woodward: 31, 105-113, 129, 135, 142, 145.
Woodward County: 30, 112, 125, 126, 130, 135.
Wyatt, Nathaniel (Zip): 21.